HANDBOOK
FOR
SERVANTS

GAYLE D. ERWIN

YAHSHUA
PUBLISHING

Handbook for Servants
Copyright © 2000 by Gayle D. Erwin
ISBN 1-56599-254-7

YAHSHUA Publishing
PO Box 219
Cathedral City, CA 92235-0219
Phone 760-321-0077
FAX 760-202-1139

Printed in the United States of America

Table of Contents

The Great Pretender

I am a pretender. I wear suspenders (braces to the British, hosentrager to the Germans or galluses if you are from Kentucky) as you may know. My unique collection of suspenders includes a number of Harley Davidson ones. People then often ask me if I ride a Harley. I tell them, "Some people's Harley goes *vroom, vroom.* Mine just goes *snap, snap.*" I also have a pair that looks like a piano keyboard. People ask me if I play the piano. I tell them, "No, but I recognize a piano when I see one."

So, now this book! The only true handbook for the Christian is the Bible; consequently, this book is a pretender though not, in any way, attempting to take the place of the Bible. I am an incurable believer.

However, having studied the servant-hearted, others-centered nature of Jesus and written about it in **The Jesus Style**, the first and most important of my books, the question of application constantly arises. Now, the real problem of the Bible condenses to interpretation. Frankly, I've met true believers with weird interpretations and weird believers with true interpretations. Hopefully, in this book of applications, I fall into the "true interpretations" category whether I manage to crawl out of "weird" or not.

You must understand that my opinions, though strongly felt and expressed, do not mean that I consider myself more spiritual or closer to God than you. Indeed, I consider that God prompts me to speak constantly about servanthood and its practicalities simply because that is the only way I will ever begin to learn for myself.

Then why write this? Simple. Not only do I believe that God has me under contract to share his nature, but he has intersected my life every inch of the way with subtle and/or dramatic experiences to open my eyes and enlarge my heart. Further, he seems to have given me a pair of eyes that see what is often missed and ears to hear shouts that others silence. Not to share what I have seen and heard with you would constitute negligence on my part. So hang on while I attempt to maintain (achieve?) innocence.

What It's All About

No thought, no philosophy, no chosen lifestyle, no technology approaches the incredible impact and influence Jesus renders in my life. Not the thought of Jesus or the concept of "the Christ", but the reality of him as a human person and as God shapes and guides every facet of my life and fiber of my being. The choice to follow Jesus with the resulting discovery of his present, personal reality and the truth of Scripture was the wisest, greatest, most effective decision of my life.

The growth of that decision meant closer study of him in the Scripture, especially the Gospels. Closer study meant seeing and understanding his attitudes in a way that launched a lifetime loyalty to his very nature. The discoveries about Jesus that shaped my life resulted, as you may know, in a book called **The Jesus Style**. Everything I have done since then—my teaching, the production of video and audio tapes, the writing of additional books including this one, the publication of newsletters and other individual writings—flows from that book and its concepts.

The overriding single understanding that boils down to the ultimate fact of life is the servant/others-centered heart of Jesus. If you understand this, you truly have life mastered. That is what it is all about. Early on in the history of the universe, the heavens divided into the servants and the self-centered. The servant side became paradise. The self-centered side formed hell. It is as simple as that.

This understanding so undergirded the actions of Jesus, he patiently spent extensive time teaching his slow-learning disciples. Indeed, the servant nature taught and lived by Jesus grates against the basic nature of man so strongly that the disciples likely resisted the teaching to the point of retardation.

Jesus left no loopholes, no uncertainty, no alternatives when he stated to the disciples in a famous encounter in the region of Caesaria Phillipi: *If any man will come after me, let him deny himself, and take up his cross and follow me.* (Matthew 16:24 KJ) It's that "self" word that bothers me the most. With the world, my nature seeks self-esteem, self-realization, self-exaltation, but my natural self never seeks servanthood. Some people choose this fact as reason to reject God. I choose to recognize that this fact means I am not God and need him desperately.

For those of you who have heard or read this message countless times, I still, without shame, repeat it once again. With some laughter, I recall a pastor saying to me, "Some people are five point Calvinists. I have become a 14-point Erwinist." I knew that he did not mean that he followed me, but that he gladly followed Jesus in the 14 points of his nature I relentlessly espouse. So, once again, here Jesus describes himself in his "greatest in the kingdom" teachings:

Servant:

- Not lord it over others
- Leadership by example
- Humble
- As a child
- As the younger
- Least
- Last
- No force
- No selfish ambition
- No reputation
- Human
- Obedient
- Death

Matthew 18:1-5,15; 20:16,20-28; 23:1-4,11-12
Mark 9:33-35; 10:43-45
Luke 9:46-48; 14:11; 22:24-27
John 13:12-17

Read it, stare at it, let him take over and do it for you.

Now, you can read the rest of this book.

Blessing

In that dramatic moment after the Children of Israel opted for a new god (a golden calf), Moses issued a call for decision to which only his own family responded. Now, the true God limited the priesthood to the sons of Aaron (Moses' brother) and the Levites—those who had responded.

The labor of the Levite, marvelously simple, consisted of carrying the Ark of the Covenant, standing before the Lord to minister and, finally, blessing the people in God's Name. Amazing. Surely their job would be to harass the people and whip them into spiritual shape, wouldn't it? Surely God's vengeance would continue to burn against this sorry lot of disloyal people!

But, No! This God of compassion, grace, patience, mercy and forgiveness instead authorized his representatives to bless the people. Amazing!

Indeed, this Lord of the universe made sure the blessing would be done right by giving careful instructions and allowing no variations. He instructed them to say:

The LORD bless you and keep you;
The LORD make his face to shine upon you,
And be gracious to you;
The LORD lift up His countenance upon you,
And give you peace. (Numbers 6:24-26 NKJ)

How utterly benevolent! No conditions—just blessing. Perhaps this Lord of Lords wanted to make sure his nature was truly known.

Sometimes, I read or hear people using another expression of blessing in letters or departures. They will write or say "Mizpah."

This comes from the moment in Genesis as Jacob and Laban, his uncle, finally part ways. Laban had chased Jacob to retrieve his own household gods, his most valuable possessions, that were now cleverly hidden by Rachel, Jacob's wife. This was a hostile parting.

Laban knew that he could no longer police the actions of Jacob, so they build a memorial and Laban said, *...The LORD watch between me and thee, when we are absent one from another.* (Genesis 31:49 KJ) What this means in "street language" is "The Lord is going to be your policeman now, you rascal, while I can't watch you."

So, you may want to be a bit careful when using that "blessing." Someone you "bless" may actually know the meaning.

In the meantime, God still instructs us to put on his nature. (Colossians 3:12-17) Often, in this day, methods of sharing the "good news" lack a sense of blessing. Instead, wrath, vengeance and hostility often accompany our communication—sort of a Mizpah rather than a Gospel. Maybe, if we understand the God we serve, it is time for Mizpah to fade and the blessing of the good news to reign.

Mizpah may produce more immediately observable results and lure us to its threat, but God calls us to blessing. The results must be in his hands. A servant is a blesser.

Grace

Nothing separates the servant from the legalist more than grace. First, the servant knows he is the recipient of grace and second, out of a grateful heart, he wishes to pass that grace along.

We readily see God's servants, lovers of people in his behalf, as channels of grace and blessing. Through servanthood, we express the absolute goodwill and blessing of God to people, even undeserving and ungrateful people. And well it should be since grace defines God's interaction with mankind more than any other single word.

John in his Gospel informs us that *the law came by Moses, grace and truth by Jesus Christ.* Now we live in a season of his favor. Favor we do not deserve, but then, that is the nature of grace.

Grace, God's unmerited favor, is so troubling to mankind. The human heart arrogantly thinks it can somehow deserve rewards by steeled will or random good actions. All religions build themselves around some form of law. The "new age" expressions, though with no moral structures that I know of, still demand certain rituals or crystals or appliances or locations to touch the spirit world. Other Eastern religions require some sacrifice, some inordinate action.

Only God offers grace and that through Jesus. So free, yet so expensive. Giving up arrogance to admit inadequacy and receive grace is most difficult. Receiving grace leaves pride (our bastion of resistance) crumbling in the dust.

Servanthood, though, renders the smile of God, enjoys the anointing of the Spirit and proves the presence of Jesus in ways that would please Paul the Apostle as he wrote of grace to the Romans as well as James as he wrote his epistle of works. The teacher of grace often receives the frowns of the legalist along with the suspicions of those who give lip service to grace, but the others-centered, servant-hearted deliverer of grace is irresistible.

Servanthood delivers a "face of grace" that says to the hesitant "I like you," and releases a child by saying "You are safe in my presence," all the while silently, but surely, honoring the Name of our Lord.

The legalist, on the other hand, requires that you serve as he conveniently escapes serving and judges your serving as being inadequate. The legalist is never satisfied. All others fall short. At a serious automobile accident, the legalist wants first to know who caused it and how we can punish him. The servant seeks to save the people.

One can do service as a legalist, but one cannot be a lover of people and be a legalist. So, servanthood and grace like "righteousness and peace" kiss each other.

Take note of these two Scripture areas that speak of the grace given to every man and the mercy that permits us ministry:

For it is by grace you have been saved, through faith—and this not from yourselves, it is the gift of God—not by works, so that no one can boast. For we are God's workmanship, created in Christ Jesus to do good works, which God prepared in advance for us to do. (Ephesians 2:8-10)

Therefore, since through God's mercy we have this ministry, we do not lose heart. Rather, we have renounced secret and shameful ways; we do not use deception, nor do we distort the word of God. On the contrary, by setting forth the truth plainly we commend ourselves to every man's conscience in the sight of God. (2 Corinthians 4:1-2)

Dealing With Manipulators

Valid and troubling questions arise for the person who chooses to follow the servant lifestyle. Once you begin to become others-centered, people might say, "Oh! So you are a slave? I have always wanted one." People will attempt to take advantage of you, to manipulate you.

Is this what servanthood means? Definitely not! Becoming a doormat and having people walk on you so you can say, "Thanks, I needed that," is a sickness rather than true servanthood.

First, let's assume, just for the talking point, that manipulation of others is a sickness (it is a sin, too). If we permit people to manipulate us or take advantage of our servanthood, then we are feeding them another spoonful of germs rather than aiding their health. True servanthood is relinquishing all rights for selfishness and choosing to do only what is right and best for others.

Let's look at this struggle from a biblical and comparison basis:

Servanthood vs. Servitude

Choice Not Force

When we choose our work, we can endure any difficulty. When we feel work has been forced upon us, we go through what is called "burnout" (to be addressed later). Jesus did good beyond the limit of paper to record (John 21:25) and Paul suffered intensely without being moved (Acts 20:24). How? They chose! Then walked in joy.

Notice the affirmation of Jesus in John 10:17-18: *The reason my Father loves me is that I lay down my life—only to take it up again. No one takes it from me, but I lay it down of my own accord. I have authority to lay it down and authority to take it up again. This command I received from my Father.* "Accord" is choice; "takes" is force. Paul adopts the same theme in 1 Corinthians 9:19: *Though I am free and belong to no man, I make myself a slave to everyone, to win as many as possible.*

"Free" means that no one had enslaved him. That would be force. "Make myself a slave" is choice.

This concept sheds light on another statement of Jesus that usually troubles us (the emphases are mine): *But I tell you, Do not resist an evil person. If someone strikes you on the right cheek* (force), *turn to him the other also* (choice). *And if someone wants to sue you and take your tunic* (force), *let him have your cloak as well* (choice). *If someone forces you to go one mile* (force), *go with him two miles* (choice). (Matthew 5:39-41)

In each case, our choice shows the contrast of two different kingdoms and achieves a remarkable and often-unnoticed victory—by our choice we actually show our oppressor that we care about him, also. This forces the oppressor into a series of unexpected considerations that might produce conversion. "Choice" is certainly a necessity to fulfill the command of Jesus to love our enemies and do good to them who mistreat us (Matthew 5:44).

So, now our chart looks like this:

SERVANTHOOD IS NOT SERVITUDE
Choice is not Force
Accord is not Takes
Make Myself Slave is not Enslaved
Turn Other Cheek is not Strike One Cheek
Go Two Miles is not Go One Mile
Give Cloak is not Take Coat

Methods of Jesus

We see several attempts in the Gospels to manipulate Jesus. Once it occurred when he finished feeding the 5000. You would think that such a miracle would have dropped what they heard from their brains to their hearts; but, no, their hearts were teflon covered and it slipped to their bellies.

17

Now they wanted to come and take Jesus by *force* and make him king.

How did Jesus handle this? He ran! He even walked on water to get away from there. Sometimes manipulation so overwhelms that our only method of dealing with it is to run—even walk on water.

Nicodemus used flattery on Jesus in their famous encounter in John 3:1,2: *There was a man of the Pharisees, named Nicodemus, a ruler of the Jews: The same came to Jesus by night, and said unto him, Rabbi, we know that thou art a teacher come from God: for no man can do these miracles that thou doest, except God be with him.* (KJ) Though he had such high thoughts about Jesus, Nicodemus still came to Jesus by night, apparently not wanting to be seen and perhaps damage his career.

Jesus' response was strange and direct, *You must be born again.* Nicodemus, on hearing that, now wants to argue with Jesus. How curious after what he said in the beginning. Nicodemus was being manipulative and Jesus confronted him.

On another occasion, Jesus confronted manipulation with a dilemma. Listen to the sweet words in Matthew 22:15-22:

> Then the Pharisees went out and laid plans to trap him in his words.
> They sent their disciples to him along with the Herodians. "Teacher," they said, "we know you are a man of integrity and

that you teach the way of God in accordance with the truth. You aren't swayed by men, because you pay no attention to who they are. Tell us then, what is your opinion? Is it right to pay taxes to Caesar or not?"

But Jesus, knowing their evil intent, said, "You hypocrites, why are you trying to trap me?

Show me the coin used for paying the tax." They brought him a denarius,

and he asked them, "Whose portrait is this? And whose inscription?"

"Caesar's," they replied. Then he said to them, "Give to Caesar what is Caesar's, and to God what is God's."

When they heard this, they were amazed. So they left him and went away.

Can you see the method of manipulation? Flattery! I'm sure Jesus recognized their duplicity instantly.

Need Binds Us

Jesus did not need to have the Pharisee tell him he was a man of integrity. He already knew. He did not need to be told that he spoke only the truth. He already knew. He did not need to be told that he was not swayed by men. He already knew.

Jesus did not need to be told by Nicodemus that he was a man come from God. He already knew. He didn't need to be told that he couldn't do these things unless God was with him. He already knew.

Whenever we need the compliments or reinforcement of men or their approval, we become dangerously subject to their manipulation and bondage. I watched a church leader, after two years of depression, fall prey to a self-proclaimed prophet. This "prophet" came telling of monstrous miracles God would produce through this leader's ministry. According to this "prophet" the depressed leader would see the greatest revival in history.

This leader so desperately needed to hear this affirmation that he was completely fooled and turned his ministry over to this "prophet." It virtually ended the leader's ministry, because none of the prophecies came true.

I have a remarkable article from "The Los Angeles Times" that relates how a new-age medium completely compromised and embarrassed several famous people (also at a time of depression in their lives) by feeding them the hogwash that in their prior lives (ah, the deception of reincarnation) they had been teachers of great people including Jesus. One of them had the candor to admit that they needed to hear that.

What prevents these personal tragedies? I know only one remedy—hear what God says to us and about us in his Word and rest lavishly in it.

Fear and Guilt

After flattery, the main tools of the manipulator are fear and guilt. Anytime someone tries to move me to actions of their choice through fear, I simply remember the words of John, ...*perfect love casts out fear,....* (1 John 4:18 NKJ) So, if you are trying to make me afraid, it means that you don't love me and it is easy to resist.

If you attempt to move me to actions of your choice through guilt, I simply remember the words of Paul, ...*there is now no condemnation* (guilt) *for those who are in Christ Jesus,....* (Romans 8:1) Armed with that reinforcement, I resist gladly.

Resistance Movement

Obviously, Jesus resisted manipulators by various means. Some he confronted. From others he ran. Manipulators reduce your choices and limit your freedom—the very opposite of the nature of Jesus. So, we see that every tool of the manipulator is negated by Scripture. Jesus wants us to be free, free to choose to do what is right and best for others.

Permit me some observations about manipulators from my own experience. As a pastor, I faced a constant barrage of people wanting to command my choices. Through the understanding of the nature of Jesus, I grew in the ability to detect when someone sought to take advantage of me. Since I am (I pray) committed to doing what is right and best for people, I learned to confront by saying something like this: "I am uncomfortable because I cannot discern what the loving thing is to do, so I must say, 'No'." This answer laid no accusations on anyone and accepted the responsibility of the decision for myself.

I also learned that a seasoned manipulator (we all are!) accepts no "no's." When they heard a "no," the next response would be to ask me, "Why?" The moment I attempted to explain my decision, all was lost. Manipulators are better at destroying my explanations than I am in coming up with them. I learned to simply relate that this was my choice.

Failing in the question of why, a good manipulator will create a scene, either by attempting to shame or shout or cause some other problem. I learned to enjoy the drama rather than be moved. Usually, such resistance on my part would "smoke out" the truth about the person's motives in their response.

Often the "scene creation" expresses itself in accusing you of not being a true Christian. After all, if you are a true Christian, wouldn't you do what they ask? (Guilt!) If you are not at rest in your relationship with the Lord, this devastates. However, such an accusation is proof of their motivation.

Picture a classic scene of a three-year-old child throwing himself on the floor of a grocery store screaming and beating his head on the floor because his mother has just refused to buy him some candy. The embarrassment causes some mothers to yield to the child's demands; but when they do, the mother has established a terrible and damaging precedent for the child. Instead, if the child is left alone in his protest, about the third time his head hits the floor, he will realize the pain and energy output is unfulfilling and will quit.

Warning Flags

Whenever I yielded to a manipulator, I experienced a disgust with myself in succumbing to them. Further responses included avoiding that person or making shifts in my relationship that would give me protection. All of these results were more unhealthy to me than resistance would be, so I have developed what I call "trip hammers" in my mind. When some inappropriate action occurs, it hits the lever and releases a rapidly waving flag in my mind that reads, "Watch out! This may be manipulation." The flags are numerous:

If you try to make me afraid...boiiiing...flag!
If you try to make me feel guilty...flag!
If you try to tap my greed...flag!
If you offer me a leap in power...flag!
If you heap flowery statements on me...flag!
If I think I will hate myself for doing this...flag!
If this will cause me to avoid you...flag!
If this grabs my ego...flag!

If you are reducing my freedom...flag!

Perhaps this is a lot of flag waving, but it has served me well.

Finally, and you must know I would come to this, I discovered that the more I stared at and prayed about the nature of Jesus, the more I could discern when attempts at manipulation were occurring. Most of all, the more I stared at the nature of Jesus, the less I wanted to manipulate others. The change in me was the most important.

Service vs. Servanthood

Once, in a meeting with a neighbor pastor of an old established church, the conversation turned to what I had been writing about, "servanthood." He let out an "aha" as if a discovery had been made and said, "You are talking about service. We are old hands at that. We have been teaching service for years and our people are tired of that." At first I didn't know what to say until it dawned on me that there was a distinct difference between service and servanthood as I was hearing him.

Service seemed to be something religious you could do that might not be a result of your own desires. Service could be a way of pigeon-holing spiritual life away from your everyday actions. Service could be a legalistic response to a desire for God's favor, a means of gaining points with God. Service could be what Paul spoke about in 1 Corinthians

13:3 when he said, ...*though I give my body to be burned, and have not charity, it profiteth me nothing.* (KJ)

This is not to infer that all service falls under the negative categories I have described. Indeed, thank God for all the energies put into his kingdom, but I must paint some contrasts.

Service can easily fall into the category of servitude in which one, though a volunteer, serves involuntarily, not out of choice but out of compulsion; whereas, servanthood flows from choosing to lay down one's life and is not manipulated into its actions.

Servanthood is a way of seeing people through the eyes of Jesus, not merely something else to do along the way. Servanthood involves an others-centered attitude that does not put life into compartments. Servanthood without bothering to think of itself as service simply is service.

Servanthood and Self Care

In my imagination, I keep seeing a self-effacing person running around, doing for others, looking a bit unkempt himself but always wearing a slightly pained do-you-see-how-much-I-am-doing look. When I think of that, I don't want to be that way. Now, the question naturally arises, "Can one serve others to the point that he destroys himself?" The answer is "yes," but it doesn't have to be.

To be a servant means to choose to do at all times what is best for others. If God has gifted you, then stewardship of his gift requires that you keep yourself best able to use that gift. If I am driven to sickness or exhaustion by my serving, I am hardly able to be the best for anyone else. True servanthood means that I care for myself physically and emotionally in a way that permits my highest and best to be presented for the use of the Master. Even Jesus took the time to rest. True, there were times he did not get to eat or was pursued by the crowds, but he often went to great lengths in order to rest and be alone with his Father. I find that I need to be alert to those internal barometers that tell me I am becoming less useful or even damaging and should seek diversion. A good servant is not compulsively driven but is, instead, wisely driven by loving choices.

Servanthood vs. Burnout

For many years I found it difficult to believe the statement by Jesus that his yoke was easy and his burden was light. A messianic complex I carried around said to me that if I didn't stay busy all the time, the church would collapse and the world would perish. Further complicating the scene was my reaction to apparent ingratitude. If people didn't notice that I was working so hard or if they appeared resistant to change, the result was predictable. I would become angry and frustrated, then fall into a hopeless tailspin to burnout.

Several things helped rescue me from those dangerous chains. First, I was challenged to see how arrogant it was to believe that the kingdom rose and fell on my actions alone. Indeed, when I began to take my hands off the church, things improved. People relaxed and worked with more joy.

Second, I saw that Jesus and Paul, though working much harder than I, seemed never to burn out. Why? It seems to me from what I read that Jesus and Paul truly enjoyed what they did. The Bible describes Jesus being beside himself with joy and Paul facing persecutions gladly. When Jesus said that obeying his commandment to love would produce full joy (John 15:11), when he left peace with the disciples (John 14:27), when he stated that whoever lost his life for Christ's sake would find it (Matthew 16:25) and that his yoke was easy and his burden light and he would give rest (Matthew 11:28,29), that seemed to be adequate evidence that working for Jesus should not produce burnout.

The key seems to be the joy and inner rest that comes from being a loving person by choice, free from the chains of compulsion and manipulation, and the peace that pervades your being when you can lay your head on your pillow at night knowing that you have harmed no one and perhaps benefited someone.

When Servanthood Fails

Sometimes servanthood simply doesn't work. In spite of all you do for people, occasionally they throw your best efforts back in your face and go about their destructive or self-willed ways. That can be terribly disappointing.

Two things have been a help to me in that area. First, I am basically serving Jesus and the things I do are for him and are not for the results alone. I am to be a "faithful" servant, not necessarily a successful one as the world judges success. I cannot read Hebrews 11 or the prophet Jeremiah without seeing that faith and obedience sometimes (perhaps often) produce actions not in keeping with success. In fact, pure pragmatism can be a demonic taskmaster—a mammon that you cannot serve along with God.

Second, there is something to be said for abandoning an unresponsive scene. Jesus didn't hesitate to instruct the apostles to leave villages that refused to receive the message. Paul commanded Timothy to pass the learning along to "faithful" men. Jesus prayed all night before he carefully chose the ones who would be nearest to him. It is not necessarily spiritual to beat our heads against a wall of resistance when so many are hungry and receptive. Servanthood also means to make the best use of our time and resources for others.

Servanthood and Ethics

Perhaps the most common problem I face in interaction with those who attempt the life of the servant is the resistance of the systems of the world to such a concept and life. Almost all organizations or institutions, however great their beginnings and purpose may be, develop certain rigidities as they grow old. The main rigidity is the "way of doing things" if you wish to survive in the system. The principles of survival are self-centered for both persons and institutions, and those principles by nature are in conflict with servanthood.

This would be a minor problem were it not for the fact that most of us "owe our souls to the company store" as the old song goes. We are employed by or so entwined with the systems of this world, be they church or business, that the question of what is best for people contrasted with what is required of us by our employer sometimes takes on enormous economic consequences.

How do you survive in the business world or in a position where the question of ethics is somewhere down the line (if in the list at all) below profits or growth.

First, I do believe that to be a servant means to be a better employee, better in a way that would earn respect or a hearing if need be. Second, as an employee, I owe loyalty to my employer and should not subvert his success. Third, I owe honesty to my employer—an honesty that says "I am loyal but you must hear how I feel about this decision and why this may be an ethical problem to me." Fourth, I should do my best to keep pressure on the system by using its own structures and whatever favor from executives may be available to me to develop a higher level of ethics and people orientation.

Often there is desire on the part of authority to be caring but creativity or incentive to do so is lacking. At this point the servant becomes most effective, since his heart is turned toward others. However, if a person is interested only in collecting his pay and going home, then his business life and his servant life will become entirely separate.

Servanthood and Emotions

The final area for this discussion of problems is the weakness of our own emotions. "Tough love" might be a better title for this section. Family relationships prove to be the biggest battleground of our emotions.

There are many peaks along the way—too many to even list, but let us look only at an example. Recently, a mother distraught over relationship with an older son shared her dilemma with me. It was time for her son to be on his own, yet he was not gainfully employed. His presence in the house was now a strain on its economy and emotions. She had made him leave once only to receive him back when he returned begging. Her motherly instincts were getting in the way of a difficult decision that would make him responsible for himself. Often, a highly charged sob story can touch us in emotional ways that blind us to the real question of what is truly best for the other person.

In my childhood years when the time came for a woodshed experience, my father would always say, "This is going to hurt me more than it hurts you, son." I didn't understand that then, but now, as a father, I do. I appreciate his discipline now, but then I used every means I could to escape—crying, pleading for mercy, etc. It was a good show, but my father was willing to hurt more than I for my own good. In these emotional areas, when you step back from them, the answer seems obvious and logical; yet, they are the most difficult to follow through. Because of his love for the rich young ruler, Jesus watched with sorrow as he walked away unrepentant. But Jesus let him go. It was the only loving thing to do.

I have come to one conclusion about servanthood—it often means making a very difficult and personally costly decision to maintain what is truly best for someone else. Sometimes, we must simply accept the sorrow of having our insides torn or melted as the situation dictates.

Thanks

Turkey Day! The TV commentator insisted as if calling it "Thanksgiving" would curl his lips into a forbidden word. No surprise. In new age self-centeredness, to say "thank you" means someone out there is greater than you and can actually do something for you.

Never assume that ingratitude is only the preserve of the rich and sophisticated, the educated and erudite. A devastating discovery that destroys many social workers is the lack of thankfulness among even the poor. It is my "right" is a frequent battle cry.

If there is one trait of human beings that proves us opposed to God, it is our belief that we are the highest, that we are little gods who need no one else. In other words, when our ego clings to the throne, when our self-centeredness rules our day, then we are most removed from God; and all manner of evil flows from us. However, just as forgiveness places us in ultimate health in relationship with other people, thankfulness may place us in ultimate he lth with God.

God certainly cannot be faulted (just as in forgiveness) for his kindness to us. Out of his overflowing grace he treats us vastly beyond our due. ...*he is kind to the ungrateful and wicked.* (Luke 6:35) Indeed, Jesus granted healing to ten lepers while probably knowing that only one (the least likely—a Samaritan) would return to offer thanks.

As I travel around the world, I am always eager to return to my homeland (though I am not blind to its problems), because no country is as blessed with convenience and creature-comforts as we are. Unfortunately, though we founded this country as refugee lepers of the world and have been favored by God's grace, we still think it is our doing. I personally wish we would change our national anthem from "bombs bursting in air" to the more appropriate "America the Beautiful" which contains the line "God shed his grace on thee." Even when I get frustrated by our bureaucracy, I am still thankful to be home and for what God has done here. Obviously God has been kind to the ungrateful, even us.

We should not be shocked. God knew about our times and informs us through the pen of Paul: *People will be lovers of themselves, lovers of money, boastful, proud, abusive, disobedient to their parents, ungrateful, unholy, without love, unforgiving, slanderous, without self-control, brutal, not lovers of the good, treacherous, rash, conceited, lovers of pleasure rather than lovers of God—....*
(2 Timothy 3:2-4)

Those who insist on rejecting God signal it quickly through ingratitude. Paul speaks again in Romans: 1:21 *For although they knew God, they neither glorified him as God nor gave thanks to him, but their thinking became futile and their foolish hearts were darkened.* God shows himself to mankind, but they refuse to give him glory. The ultimate end is a destroyed mind. I prefer thankfulness.

The Perfect Path

Simple reading of Scripture leads us to a life of thanksgiving. Simple relationship with God fills us with thanksgiving. Who among us has not sung or memorized the psalmist's entry level approach to God: *Enter his gates with thanksgiving and his courts with praise; give thanks to him and praise his name.* (Psalms 100:4) Perhaps thanksgiving and praise are so intertwined that we cannot separate them. Perhaps thanksgiving unlocks additional doors of God's blessing. Listen again to the Psalms: 50:23 *He who sacrifices thank offerings honors me, and he prepares the way so that I may show him the salvation of God.*

God works so powerfully in our lives that, regardless of the circumstances we experience, we can be grateful people. The circumstances will not be the source of our gratitude; our God and our response to him fuels thanks. Paul clarifies that in an often misinterpreted passage: *...give thanks in all circumstances, for this is God's will for you in Christ Jesus.* (1 Thessalonians 5:18)

Perfect Reminders

Before Jesus fed the multitude, even he gave thanks. If anyone was qualified to be arrogant and unthankful, it would be Jesus. However, in setting the example for us, his own heart overflowed with thanksgiving. Then, in beginning the meal that would feed the memory of millions, Jesus gave thanks, broke the bread and told us this was his body. Little wonder that Paul names the cup that follows, the cup of thanksgiving: *Is not the cup of thanksgiving for which we give thanks a participation in the blood of Christ? And is not the bread that we break a participation in the body of Christ?* (1 Corinthians 10:16)

Communion is a thanksgiving. How can I remember Jesus without exploding with gratitude? I embarrass myself sometimes in the presence of others with a "Thank you, Jesus" that cannot be contained within my skin as I ponder his grace.

Communion is not the only symbol of our gratitude. If I hear the words that the 120 spoke on the Day of Pentecost correctly and read Corinthians accurately, it appears that the main use of the gift of tongues is for thanksgiving. When Paul draws boundaries for its public use, note his description: *If you are praising God with your spirit, how can one who finds himself among those who do not understand say "Amen" to your thanksgiving, since he does not know what you are saying? You may be giv-*

ing thanks well enough, but the other man is not edi-fied. (1 Corinthians 14:16,17)

Perfect Overflow

Thanksgiving produces practical benefits that make our membership in the kingdom of God better than any other membership we have. Thanksgiving:

1. Cleanses our food.
1 Timothy 4:3,4 *They forbid people to marry and order them to abstain from certain foods, which God created to be received with thanksgiving by those who believe and who know the truth. For everything God created is good, and nothing is to be rejected if it is received with thanksgiving.*

2. Strengthens our faith.
Colossians 2:7 *...rooted and built up in him, strengthened in the faith as you were taught, and overflowing with thankfulness.*

3. Reduces our anxiety.
Philippians 4:6 *Do not be anxious about anything, but in everything, by prayer and petition, with thanksgiving, present your requests to God.*

4. Makes every day God's.
Romans 14:6 *He who regards one day as special, does so to the Lord. He who eats meat, eats to the Lord, for he gives thanks to God; and he who*

abstains, does so to the Lord and gives thanks to God.

5. Keeps peace.
Colossians 3:15 *Let the peace of Christ rule in your hearts, since as members of one body you were called to peace. And be thankful.*
1 Timothy 2:1,2 *I urge, then, first of all, that requests, prayers, intercession and thanksgiving be made for everyone—for kings and all those in authority, that we may live peaceful and quiet lives in all godliness and holiness.*

6. Gives access to God.
Colossians 3 :17 *And whatever you do, whether in word or deed, do it all in the name of the Lord Jesus, giving thanks to God the Father through him.*

7. Flows from generosity.
2 Corinthians 9:11 *You will be made rich in every way so that you can be generous on every occasion, and through us your generosity will result in thanksgiving to God.*

8. Recognizes our future.
Hebrews 12:28 *Therefore, since we are receiving a kingdom that cannot be shaken, let us be thankful and so worship God acceptably with reverence and awe,....*

Since thanksgiving reaps such benefits and focuses attention on God himself and imitates Jesus and causes overflow (symbolic of the Holy Spirit in John 7) and improves me, what is left for me to say?

Thank you, thank you, thank you!

Defending Jesus

Brave mockers try through the centuries. Modern media suppresses. Every attempt is made to paint Jesus in a bad light. Some truly succeed, but their success simply guarantees that they all fail. No matter how you speak of Jesus, the simple fact that you speak of him causes him to win.

In the rock opera "Jesus Christ Superstar," the writers viewed Jesus through the eyes of Judas. This focus caused many inaccuracies and misrepresentations; however, I am convinced that this rock opera was a major contributor to that revival we call "The Jesus Movement." In whatever manner you speak of Jesus, he wins.

The movie made of that musical "Jesus Christ Superstar" closes with the theatrical crew leaving the desert set and pausing, each one of them, to look back in deep thought at the three crosses still standing as part of their set. That scene alone was enough to grip all but the hardest of hearts. However we portray him, something reaches the depths of our being and yells, "He is Truth."

His Truth overpowers even in his silence. On trial before the governor named Pilate, Jesus had no defense lawyers. The prosecution had it all with many witnesses. All the witnesses in that trial gave negative reports about Jesus. Though they conflicted in their accounts, they were unanimous in their hostility. Yet, after viewing all these terrible pictures of Jesus, Pilate's declaration matches the cry of my own heart, ...*I find in him no fault at all.* (John 18:38 KJ) The result of all the negatives was "no fault."

Two thieves hanging beside Jesus joined the crowds in mockery of him until one, overcome by reality, declares the innocence of Jesus and asks for forgiveness. What changed the mind of the thief? Perhaps his own repeated blasphemy sunk the Name into his heart. Jesus won.

Peter and John plunked an item of great value into the can of a beggar when they invited him, *In the Name of Jesus Christ of Nazareth, rise up and walk.* The ensuing charade brought a warning from the authorities. It was not a warning about healing people. The problem was the Name. "Don't use it," they warned. Jesus was winning.

Paul, in a statement far beyond my maturity, relates that some preach Christ for selfish ambition, some to make trouble for Paul, some for envy and rivalry, some insincerely and with false motives. Yet he glories in the simple fact that Christ is preached. Amazing. Perhaps he knew from his own experience that simply hearing that Name over and over produces victory.

After the televangelist scandals of the late 1900s, in a radio interview I was asked if I thought their actions had damaged the kingdom. I responded, "No." First of all, they, by manifesting their humanity, purified the kingdom. Second, beyond all the shame and embarrassment, these men spoke of Jesus, the one who forgives people who do such bad things. I don't believe the connection was lost in the minds of people. Third, any who came to know the Lord because of them would have no trouble separating what they did from the Truth of their Savior. Jesus always wins!

The European atheists of a few centuries ago blasted Jesus and the Bible every chance they could. Now, the house of one of them is used to print Bibles. Their attacks merely served to keep his Name before the people.

The Beatles, great singing group of the last century, declared themselves to be bigger than Jesus. Apparently, that did not upset Jesus. You don't need to confront pride; you only need to let it have its way. Pride doesn't have to be attacked. It collapses from its own weight. Now, the Beatles' last gasp is considerably less than messianic.

On a plane that had a stop in Las Vegas, I noticed that it was made up of a tour group and had become a party plane. For some reason, they took up with me, so I whooped with them. After they had settled down, I walked toward the back of the plane. The ringleader of the group called me over and asked, "Hey, mister. What do you do for a living?"

"I have more fun than anybody," I told him.

"I believe you," he responded.

"I go all over the world teaching on the nature of Jesus," I continued.

His hand slapped his forehead as he exclaimed, "Oh my god! You just ruined my weekend."

"What did I do?" I asked.

"You said that Name, Jesus. I am on my way to Las Vegas looking for women and you had to say that Name, Jesus. Now I have to think about this again." Just the Name reached something deep in this man.

A movie called "The Last Temptation of Christ" drew heavy negative response from the Church with people even picketing the producer and carrying hostile signs. Our response guaranteed the financial success of the movie. Reviewers called it a dud, but our advertising sent flocks to see it. Were people fooled? No! They knew this was not true about Jesus. However, the film brought Jesus' Name before the people. A friend of mine was asked by a Jewish friend to go with her to see the film and explain the errors about Jesus. Jesus wins.

The media tries hard to remove the Name of Jesus from Christmas, though it is his own season. They want to merely refer to it as a "holiday." Holiday is short for "holy day." Holy? Who is holy? Jesus still wins.

Every automobile that drives on this continent and in many other places carries a simple witness to Jesus. They all contain a date, i.e., 2000, 2005. That is 2000 AD! AD! In the year of our Lord! Who is our Lord from whom this date comes and whose birth it marks? Jesus wins again.

When people curse, they do not choose to yell, "Buddha" or "Krishna," or "Allah." No, the Name of our Lord comes out. Aha! Even in blasphemy, he wins.

When hospitals and schools are named, how many are named in honor of false gods? I can't think of a one. However, I lost count of the schools, hospitals and other institutions that somehow incorporate his Name or were founded in his Name. Why would they do that? Only because false gods do not inspire such benevolence. But Jesus does. He wins again.

I confess to inner pain at the abuse of his Name. I want to stop mouths or present an argument at best or invoke fire from Heaven at worst. I realize that some will never believe. Some will always mock. But as I sit at his feet, listening and watching, to my eternal gratitude, I know who he is in my life. He is the winner.

So, go ahead and misuse his Name if your heart is turned that way. The only damage will be to yourself and perhaps sensitive souls around you. But if you think you are damaging Jesus, don't get proud. Check the scoreboard.

Communion

Power and grace flow in this act we call "communion." Power comes because the Holy Spirit is involved in pointing us to Jesus and helping us live right. Grace flows as we attach ourselves to his goodness. Let's see if we can take some positions on the grace side of the fence.

> For I say unto you, I will not any more eat thereof, until it be fulfilled in the kingdom of God. And he took the cup, and gave thanks, and said, Take this, and divide it among yourselves: For I say unto you, I will not drink of the fruit of the vine, until the kingdom of God shall come. And he took bread, and gave thanks, and brake it, and gave unto them, saying, This is my body which is given for you: this do in remembrance of me. Likewise also the cup after supper, saying, This cup is the new testament in my blood, which is shed for you. (Luke 22:16-20 KJ)

First, many traditions exceed the authority of the Bible; thus victims of tradition abound. When Jesus began communion, his only commands were to do it and to do it to remember him. Some churches and theologies punish people by refusing to offer communion to them; however, it should not be refused to anyone who wants to remember Jesus. Never forget how Jesus treated Judas!

Some churches limit administration of communion to special authorities or to special buildings. Jesus placed no such limitation. Communion belongs to the people, not to the elite. Communion is for anyone who wants to remember and honor Jesus. The very life and action of Jesus proved that. This is why "common people" heard him gladly.

Second, the very act of participating in communion identifies you with the kingdom of God and symbolizes the continuing forgiveness of sin that Jesus offers. *For this is my blood of the new testament, which is shed for many for the remission of sins.* (Matthew 26:28 KJ) If in your heart you want to be his and are sorry for your own sins and wish to be cleansed of them, you have every reason to want to partake in communion. Communion reminds you that Jesus accepts you and keeps on forgiving.

Third, communion is a celebration of what Jesus has already done, not what we have or are doing. That fact is the joy of the New Testament. Righteousness is beyond our achievement, so Jesus provided it for us by his death and resurrection. Now, all we have to do is believe on him, accept his grace and we are "in." This calls for a party! Yes, we call the party "communion." Communion is the "Whoopee!" of living for God. I ache when I see churches turn it into some somber, sad moment. To remember the gracious, forgiving Jesus sets fireworks off in my heart. If anyone ever chooses to remember me, I hope they do it with joy and laughter. I think Jesus wants the same.

Fourth, communion is not a *reward* for having reached a certain age or joined a certain church. It is simply the memory having a party over Jesus. It is a declaration of whose side you are on. It is a smile that remains when all the rest of ourselves has disappeared (I borrow from Alice in Wonderland). Communion is for anyone who wants to say, "I believe and I belong." It is not limited to those in good standing in some institution of religion. Often people ask me at what age they should permit their children to participate in communion. The answer is simply, "At whatever age you want them to remember Jesus."

Fifth, some churches practice what is called "closed communion." They permit no one except members of their group/denomination or local church to partake with them. By this act they recognize only themselves as Christians. This is dangerously close to partaking *unworthily* which Paul warned against in 1 Corinthians 11 by not discerning or recognizing the body of Christ. How sad it is when people pull their cloaks around them and shut themselves away from the awesome, growing body of Christ in the world. How dangerous, too, since we drink *judgment on ourselves* with such exclusivity.

Sixth, I have been in conferences where some church officials of high standing were present. They were free to participate in all parts of the meeting except communion. I realized that this moment was a watershed. If they partook in any communion except from their own hands, they were admitting that others beside themselves were saved and had direct access to God. In spite of all the talk of getting together or calling us "separated brethren," until they take communion officially from us, they don't recognize us as Christians and they don't recognize what we do as communion.

Seventh, people have asked me if we should let nonbelievers participate in communion and I have heard preachers urge nonbelievers to refuse to participate. Why would a nonbeliever want to participate, anyway? Who are we to tell them not to, anyway? Maybe this is the nonbeliever's way of saying, "I now believe." I have come to the conclusion that by the grace of God, I will never say, "No." I want to keep the hand of invitation extended. If we have the keys to the kingdom, let us use them to open up the door not lock it. Freely we have received, let us freely give.

Eighth, people ask how often we should partake in communion. Churches have even split over whether it was to be weekly, monthly, quarterly. I don't know the answer to that. Jesus didn't say. He only said that as often as we do it, do it in remembrance of him. Maybe we should do it as often as we wish to remember him. Hmm.

Ninth, the Early Church in Corinth violated the use of communion seriously. So seriously that Paul warned them that they would be condemning themselves and that many of them had become sick, weak and had even died because of their misuse of communion. (1 Corinthians 11:17-34) It was not because the wrong hands administered or because they let nonbelievers participate. Rather, it was because they were not recognizing who their brothers and sisters were. Paul told them to examine themselves, i.e., look into their hearts and see whom they were excluding from the kingdom or their brotherhood. Any time we don't recognize our brothers, we maim the body of Christ. Communion should be a time of repairing our relationships. One cannot "remember Jesus" without hearing him say, ...*love one another; as I have loved you,...* (John 13:34-35 KJ)

Finally, communion rings the bells of our expectancy. It reminds us that Jesus is returning and we will do this again with him at a great banquet. What a healing to our hearts!

Hopefully you can now see that Jesus is God's open door with a smiling, welcoming face. The table behind him is ready. Welcome to the party! Let's eat!

Prayer

If you can imagine the sermon on the subject of prayer, I think I have heard it. If you have heard of the book on prayer, I think I have it in my library. Many times, the subject of prayer is made attractive by describing its power and biblical basis, while, at the same time, made unavailable by the approach. For instance:

"For power in prayer, one hour is the minimum!"

"For power in prayer, physical discomfort is necessary to keep you awake."

"For power in prayer, you must 'travail' as a woman in childbirth."

"For power in prayer, you need to be on a mountain or in a cubbyhole."

"For power in prayer, you must pray loudly (quietly, together, etc.)."

All of these prior requirements push prayer further from me. Sometimes I lose track of which rule might be missing.

Once, while speaking at a conference in what was then Rhodesia, now Zimbabwe, the customary pre-program prayer of the speakers was intersected by an interesting cultural experience. Being one of only two speakers from the USA, I was considered to "know all things" about American religious culture.

As I approached the room, several of the other speakers from Africa came rushing to ask me what was going on. They led me to the room where we normally prayed. In it was a choir from a school in the USA that would be singing in the evening session. My friends said, "Look at that. Listen to that. What is going on?" As I peeked in to see the source of the sound, I assured them that everything was OK. They were simply observing a cultural form of prayer from one segment of American church life. The choir continued to scream and beat the air like boxers as they faced the wall in a back-to-center circle.

"But why do they look so unhappy...so agonized?" I assured them that it was all part of their cultural approach and that nothing was basically "wrong" with the people. They simply had a narrow model of what prayer could be.

Prayer does not have to be narrowed by guilt, fear, program or culture.

Apparently, Jesus did not overtly display his prayer life which prompted the apostles to ask him to teach them how to pray. Could it be that Jesus' conversations with his Father were so natural the apostles didn't even notice that he was praying? Could it be that his most intensive moments with the Father were private ones when he escaped to lonely places and the disciples couldn't find him?

Surely prayer is part of God's attempt to restore the fellowship of Eden when he walked with Adam in the cool of the evening. I doubt that the conversation in the garden included much of what we now call prayer. Would Adam have yelled at God? Would Adam have screamed for God to come near? Would Adam have bowed his head and closed his eyes to validate the conversation? I think not!

We know that God is closer to us than a brother. Indeed, through the Holy Spirit he dwells in us. What, in that scenario, guides our relationship and our form of prayer? We know from Jesus that God is not impressed with repetition as a method nor is he responsive to Prayers for public consumption or as an expression of arrogance or greed. What then might he want?

Surely, he simply wants us to talk to him. The closeness and fellowship we sense with God is experienced through the method of conversation we use with him. I expect God wants us to be honest in our prayer and comfortable in our own language. I don't think fellowship with God requires some sort of physical posturing in order to be effective. I'm sure that he appreciates our believing that he is and that he is waiting to reward our belief.

From the words of Jesus, we know that God cares about "private time" with us (*closet*) and promises to reward us for that. It is also obvious that he wants us to understand and honor him as God, to submit ourselves to him (*thy kingdom come*) and to seek his intervention in our world.

God obviously doesn't want us to approach him greedily (*daily bread*) and does want us to adopt his attitude of forgiveness toward others. He wants us to be concerned about anything that would break our fellowship and be willing to communicate with him (*deliver us from evil*). Jesus' teaching on prayer is a glorious model of simplicity. Finally, if I read Jesus correctly, God wants us to pray in keeping with what Jesus would pray (*in my name*).

So, what should our conclusions be? What physical position should I be in when I pray? Any position you wish.

At what volume should I pray? At whatever volume you feel is "close."

Where should I pray? Wherever you are.

How long should I pray? For as long as you want to talk to your creator and best friend, perhaps *without ceasing.*

How big a group should I be in to pray effectively? Never even mentioned as a requirement. When Jesus used the prayer closet as an example, he certainly was promoting private prayer. Jesus himself prayed alone most of the time. The closest you can come to group prayer instructions is the *two or three agree as touching anything* or the examples of the early church.

Isn't there something I can do to improve my chances of prayer being answered? Not likely. God is hard to fool. Just love him and let him love you.

Will he listen to me if I'm not perfect? God has a centuries-long track record of listening to people with mixed motives. If you are talking to him, it is a good indication that your heart is turned his direction. The beautiful thing about prayer is that it moves you to be more like him.

Doesn't this make prayer too simple and childlike?

Amen, amen, amen!

Humor

Humor is founded in childlikeness. When Jesus told us to humble ourselves as a child, his primary goal was the honest self-assessment that is the foundation of humility. That resultant humility points out our absurdity, our "poverty of spirit," and frees us from arrogance and enables us to approach ourselves and others with the laughing freedom of a child.

But we have always been just a little reserved about the use of humor in the church and properly so. Freud was correct in his assessment of humor. He stated that all humor is hostile. In other words, in order for a joke to be funny, it has to have a brunt, someone who is humiliated or made to suffer. There is truth to that. Just check all the jokes you know. Is there someone who is the humiliated object? Look at all the various types of "ethnic" category jokes: Aggie jokes, Italian jokes, moron jokes, Pollock jokes, Portugee jokes, van der Merwe jokes.

Though it is not politically correct to even print those names, you get the point. These are joke-types that I have heard around the world. Racial jokes of any type demand that someone be put down. This is all the reason we need in the church to be wary of how we use humor.

Humor is a major part of my teaching. Maintaining consistency with the nature of Jesus demands that I resolve the obvious disparity in the use of humor. I propose to do that with the following statements.

Humor At It's Worst

- Humor that is directed at others. Since humor's basic hostility is counter to the grace we wish to deliver to people, it is important that if anyone must be the brunt of humor, it should be the speaker/deliverer of the humor.
- Humor that depends only on joke telling. Joke telling is (as I indicated above) profoundly weakened by its hostility. Telling jokes is the realm of the stand-up-comedian and that realm has removed all limits on taste and control. Further, jokes rarely translate into other languages or cultures. I have seen translators with a pained look trying to rescue some American's joke. Fortunately, telling jokes is only one kind of humor. There are safer forms that are much more illustrative and appreciated.
- Humor that is off-color. I squirm with others when inappropriate humor enters the scene. People become uncomfortable and look furtively at each other wondering what to do. Never let humor discomfort people because of its color. An "idea" taught may discomfort people, but humor

accompanying it must be a source of comfort and learning and not anxiety.

Humor At It's Best

- Humor that is life-centered. By taking normal life, seeing the humor, then expressing it, people learn while having fun. I rarely use humor just for humor's sake (though I think of funny things far more often than I can use them), instead I try to use humor as a handle and memory aid which I will discuss later.
- Humor that pours oil on troubled waters. I realized one day that the intensity of the message on the nature of Jesus was such that if I did not deliver with the relief of humor, it would be too much for people to take. That which is overwhelming is made palatable by delivering with humor.
- Humor that serves as a memory aid. Because I do not tell jokes but instead relate the humor to a specific theme or thought I want people to remember, I discover that, indeed, it works. Because the material is so positively associated and the humor so integrated, remembrance comes easy. Often I have people relate all the points of a teaching of mine that they heard years earlier because it was so easy for them to remember the relationships.
- Humor that is directed at ourselves. I have discovered several things about this method. First, when you are secure enough to be laughed at, it

defuses people's resistance. Second, when people can laugh at you, they can then laugh with you. Third, to make yourself the brunt of the humor does not lessen you in the minds of people, instead they consider you to be a "safe" person.

- Humor through slapstick. This is humor that comes from exaggerated bodily motion including facial expressions. Though it makes one look foolish, it does not actually translate as foolishness to a crowd. Humor can also be normal bodily motion in obviously funny situations. Children, as well as adults, readily respond to such humor. In fact, a properly humorous style that does not create anxiety in an audience is so well received by children that often churches release the children from Sunday School and bring them in to my teachings because they know the children will listen. I have also learned that when children are listening to you, everyone is listening to you.

- Humor as puns. Good word plays are subtle but are a compliment to an audience rather than a putdown. The weakness is that puns, like regular jokes, do not translate into other languages. Add physical motion and puns to life-centered humor and you can be wildly funny and effective at the same time.

Obviously, the above statements do not exhaustively cover humor, but they express my basic standards. Humor, unfortunately, has become so infected by our culture and carnality that we must take it through an extensive ritual of purification before it becomes edifying. That purifying demands much thinking and examination and attitude adjustment, but the power of humor makes the trial worthwhile. In many ways, humor can be an expression of grace, that great "smile of God." My prayer is that I will never turn it into a frown.

Anger

The question is not "Do you get angry?" but "How many times today have you been angry?" Amazing how life and anger walk hand in hand.

We learned early to recognize in our own babies the cry that came from need and the cry that came from anger. Married couples need only a few hours of marriage to discover this thing called anger. Unmarried people sometimes choose to remain that way because of anger. A simple drive to work, especially on a freeway, will introduce you to anger. My wife stays amused at the one-way conversations I carry on with other drivers.

Any of the talk shows on radio or TV grab your anger and give it no place to go. You hear relentless, unresolveable anger.

So what are we to do? Should we embrace and celebrate anger or solve it as a problem?

Stories of anger permeate the Scripture. God's anger burned against individuals and against the Jews in the Old Testament. We see Jesus experiencing anger in the New Testament, but where are the lessons for us? I will save that for later while we examine our own anger.

I learn a lot from the Apostles, though not always in the positive sense. In Luke 9, when Jesus and his gang were headed toward Jerusalem, though to the accompaniment of much tension, they traveled through Samaria. Time came to spend the night. Jesus sent a couple of them into a village to find a place, but they faced rejection because they were Jews headed toward Jerusalem. No love relationship existed between Jews and Samaritans.

When they reported the bad news back to the troop, James and John, expressing their anger, asked for permission to call fire down on the village just like Elijah. How is that for apostolic evangelism? Jesus rebuked them and led them to another village, reminding them that he came to save not to destroy.

I chuckle at these sons-of-thunder guys until I realize that I am just like them. I often find myself filled with nationalistic anger over some slight I perceived toward my own country without pausing to realize that I am a pilgrim and a stranger in this world, "just passin' through." Any nationalistic anger I feel is a repudiation of my heavenly citizenship.

After a flight that seemed endless and brought me into a country in the very early hours of the morning, the weariness of the trip was compounded by lines that now stretched toward passport control. Their computers decided to take the night off, so the lines inched (or millimetered) insufferably. After about two hours of waiting, another plane landed and the passengers began to gather in the line behind us, except for one man who pushed down between the lines and shoved right in front of me.

Well, I am a non-violent man, but I certainly have a voice. "You can't do that mister. Go back to the end of the line with the rest of your plane!" He ignored me. I repeated, "Mister, you can't do this...." Again, he ignored me. When it was obvious that he had established his position, he turned and beckoned toward the back of the line and his family of 12 joined him. I seethed. Weariness and anger are not comfortable companions.

Four hours into the landing, when I had finally cleared customs and was on a bus to my next destination, the Lord got my attention and whispered, "Hey, Gayle. Tough scene back there wasn't it?"

"Yes. Did you see what that man did to me back there?"

"I did and it was not very nice of him."

"It made me very angry."

"I know."

"Well, you would be too, wouldn't you?"

"Let me ask you one question? How would you have felt if he had pushed down between those rows and shoved in front of someone in the other line?"

"Well, that's life. Probably needed to learn a lesson."

"So you were angry only because he got in front of you."

"Yes."

"That's what I thought. See you later."

Busted! My anger was totally self-centered.

Regardless of why I might be angry, knowing I perhaps shouldn't be does little to assist me in overcoming it.

Anger is so dangerous that Jesus pushes it to the level of capital punishment. *But I say unto you, That whosoever is angry with his brother without a cause shall be in danger of the judgment: and whosoever shall say to his brother, Raca, shall be in danger of the council: but whosoever shall say, Thou fool, shall be in danger of hell fire.* (Matthew 5:22 KJ)

So, if anger is such a problem, how do we handle it; and why were Jesus and God, the Father, angry? Searching for that answer led me to some amazing discoveries.

I am convinced of the servant-hearted, others-centered nature of Jesus, so his anger creates some tension in my mind. How does anger fit into that nature? Understanding hit me. Jesus exhibited anger only in behalf of others. Conversely, I exhibit anger when someone gets in *my* way.

When Jesus' anger burned at the Pharisees in the synagogue of Capernaum, it was because they cared nothing for the man with the withered hand who was about to be healed on the Sabbath, only for their traditions and their power. When Jesus turned over the tables in the Temple, it was not because they were selling—the sales of animals and changing of money were genuine services to the people—but because they had developed a monopoly and were gouging people, which prevented worship and prayer rather than serving.

Jesus expressed his anger toward the apostles, when they were restraining mothers from bringing their children to him to bless them. Again, his expression was in behalf of others. How perfectly that fits with his nature and how thoroughly that shames me in mine.

When the Bible exhorts me to *be angry and sin not,* I am urged to learn to match my angers to that of Jesus and away from the source of all sin—my self-centeredness. When the Bible tells me not to let the sun go down on my anger, I am urged to grab the insight about my folly before anger becomes bitterness whose roots stay and grow and grow.

If I could learn to be angry only when Jesus is angry and be at ease when he is, life would be much better for me.

Rage

Unfortunately, we see frequently a new level of the expression of anger—rage. We are all familiar with the school shootings that have occurred in the USA and around the world, and we are all deeply hurt. Add to that, violence in the workplace, at home, in gang action that also fills our news. Everyone asks the question, "Why did they do it?" Television and newspapers have done everything they can to confuse the issue. It boils down to the fact that a person given little or no limits to his anger will find that his self-centeredness finds no fulfillment. Since "I want" is unsatisfied and limits are unlearned, the results are rage where selfishness meets its final fulfillment. The one cause no one seems to have mentioned is demon possession. Ultimate lack of self-control is a defining mark of demon possession.

The Answers

Since the Bible tells us to be angry and sin not, let's assume that anger is a very dangerous emotion and should even be considered a sin. That unlocks our best answer. Confessing our anger immediately depletes it's power over us and permits God to do his healing by forgiving us and cleansing us from unrighteousness.

Second, the great anger beater is forgiveness. When I forgive, I also give up the right to be angry. The person I forgive becomes the object of my mercy rather than my rage or vengeance. Whom I do not forgive becomes my controller. Freedom from most bondage (including anger) is wrapped in this secret healing ingredient called forgiveness.

The third way to make anger profitable is to immediately pray for the person at whom you are angry. The only warning is that you must pray for them the same kind of prayer you want prayed for yourself.

Fourth, anger, by its very nature, creates adrenaline. That adrenaline in us creates energy which looks for an outlet. For some people, that outlet is physical violence. For others it is emotional violence. There is nothing wrong in having some system of profitable exercise (a good time to mow the lawn) to deal with the real physical problem. I am convinced that the jogging craze in America has handled more adrenaline than we know.

Finally, if you find your temper on the quick side, then keep yourself constantly exposed (keep the veil pulled) to God so he can shine his glory on you and change you into his likeness. (2 Corinthians 3:18)

> Be ye angry, and sin not: let not the sun go down upon your wrath: (Ephesians 4:26 KJ)

> For a bishop must be blameless, as the steward of God; not self-willed, not soon angry, not given to wine, no striker, not given to filthy lucre; (Titus 1:7 KJ)

Politics and the Leaven of Herod

Jesus issued the warning, *...beware...the leaven of Herod.* (Mark 8:15 KJ) Yes, he warned of other leavens—Pharisees, Sadducees, Scribes—but the leaven of Herod gets ignored. We can ignore it no longer.

While the Pharisees (fundamentalists) and the Sadducees (liberals) represented the extremes of the religious world (against which Jesus warned), Herod symbolized the political world. Actually we have violated all of the leaven warnings of Jesus, but strange companions have been uncovered in the bedroom of Herod. In the day of Jesus, the Sadducees, from what we might call a "liberal" stance, had chosen to make some political compromises with the ruling country of Rome. As a result, Rome decreed that the chief priest would be a Sadducee. Thus, the political bedfellows were Herod and the Sadducees.

Today, we have kicked those liberals out (Herod is safely still in bed) and we conservatives (Pharisees?) have crawled under the sheets in the political arena. Why did we do that? Simply because we believed that the salvation of our country depended on our ability to rope the raging bull of political power and get him in our corral.

Our Man

The dream was clear: We must get "our man" in office, then everything will be all right.

We had set the stage well. Books like **The Power and the Glory** by Peter Marshall and our frequent preaching of the theme, *...if my people, who are called by my name, will humble themselves and pray and seek my face and turn from their wicked ways, then will I hear from heaven and will forgive their sin and will heal their land,* (2 Chronicles 7:14) had led us to believe that we were the new *chosen people* and that the United States had replaced Israel as the central focus of the Bible. The implications that followed were obvious:

If the United States were the new *promised land* and *God's Chosen*, then, like the Pharisees and Sadducees, we must do something about Herod. Back then the Pharisees despised Herod. The Sadducees compromised with him, and other major groups such as the Zealots (radical activists) fought with him, and the Essenes (monastics) withdrew from him. The Zealots still fight; the Essenes still withdraw; the Sadducees lick their wounds of diminished power; but now the Pharisees are doing the compromising with Herod.

Americans have placed their hopes in various Christian presidents. I have heard many stories of their spiritual commitment and dedication to biblical standards. Stories abounded of who became Christian by walking what aisle, of who prayed with whom, of the sincerity of voice when prayer was requested, of who was pastor of whom.

The question is not whether all of the above stories are true. I'm sure they are. The question is whether we should put our hope in Herod—any of our hope—even just a tiny bit, like leaven. Each president, regardless of his commitment to Christ, has failed to place us at the right hand of God and failed to place us in dominion over the world. What a pity. It wasn't because we didn't try hard enough.

I have never seen such frenzied and unquestioning political activity on the part of church people, all of it built around the argument, "When we take over, or when our man gets in, we will turn this country around and have utopia."

Now, (would you believe it?) there are even theologies preaching that *we* should be the Herod. This theology flies several banners: Dominion Theology, Kingdom Now Theology, Restoration Theology. The bottom line of these approaches is that we Christians should take over all the power centers (financial, governmental, etc.) of the world and establish the kingdom of God so Jesus can come back and reign. They must think that this great thing we call the Church is better qualified, organized and trained to be the Herod than any of our presidents were. It seems that I hear the mother of James and John asking for some special privilege for her good boys again. Somehow we think that power corrupts everyone else, but we are in a special category. We never learn.

Pilgrim's Progress

The Bible is filled with Scriptures that should give us pause before we plunge headlong into redemption by world power. Jesus informed Pilate that his kingdom was *not of this world* else his followers would fight. (John 18:36 KJ)

When Jesus told us we should be as the *younger,* (Luke 22:26 KJ) he was placing us in the category of pilgrim, even rebel. The younger was one who had little or no stake in the system of the world. The status quo was not his friend. We have abandoned that stance in order to become as the elder brother. We now wish to be the establishment.

Jesus died *outside the gate* in shame. (Hebrews 13:11-13) We want to live inside the gate in honor. *Here we do not have an enduring city....* (Hebrews 13:14) but we are trying to prove the Scripture wrong and build our enduring city now. We are no longer *looking for a city that is to come.* (Hebrews 13:14) We have decided that that city is now in the United States and we get to build it.

Isaiah learned a lesson appropriate for our day. Uzziah may have been Isaiah's hero and candidate for messiah, but then a terrible thing happened—Uzziah died! (Isaiah 6) Then Isaiah records his incredible vision that resulted. *In the year*

Uzziah died, I saw the Lord.... At that same time, he also saw himself and his people as having unclean lips and needing help from the altar of heaven. I hope I can see this lesson clearly. What failure of politicians has caused us to finally see the Lord.

So, What Now?

So, having said all of this, what is my answer? It is too simple. We are people of hope and our hope is in Jesus and him alone. If our hope is in this life, as Paul reveals, we are most miserable; but we are people of a different kingdom whose rules the world cannot understand and whose establishment waits a returning king. In the meantime, the king rules in our hearts and in our actions.

We are to be a people who are not fooled by any of Herod's seductive ways. We can even be brave enough (as Jesus was) to say to a threatening Herod, "Tell that Fox" that we will go on healing and doing the work of God's kingdom until we reach our goal. (Luke 13:32) We will focus our attention on Jesus himself and do all we can to make his Name known. We will refuse to be identified by any party or power of our day. We are his.

Does this mean we must have nothing to do with politics? Not at all. We must be as good as we can and as involved as we must for this day, but never lose our understanding that we are not people whose destiny is "this day."

The rules of the political world have not changed:

Rule 1. Get in power.

Rule 2. Stay in power.

Rule 3. Increase your power.

The power to wash feet, to serve, is an afterthought, if a thought at all.

We must never hope that any of the systems of this world carry an ounce of redemption for us. I often told my students that maturity was simply being disillusioned and handling it wisely and that I prayed they would be disillusioned quickly so they would place faith in only God himself. Hopefully, we remain disillusioned by the political world, and our hearts long for the government to be *upon his shoulder.* Perhaps now, we will reaffirm our commission to win the world one soul at a time.

In the meantime, let us *fix our eyes on Jesus.* (Hebrews 12:2)

Who God Uses

The whole realm of the heroic hinges on cultural values. American heroes, now usually sportsmen, are the biggest, the fastest, the meanest. Or they are heroes of the silver screen—the prettiest, the handsomest, the shapeliest. About the only other heroes left are the richest. Military and ethical heroes are in short supply. Oh, ethical heroes exist but no one knows who they are. Every culture adopts a similar form. The heroic degrades as rapidly as the moral structure of a society.

What about the heroes of the servant? Might they be different? If I read Scripture correctly, they are vastly different. Perhaps they could even be called God's heroes, certainly servant clients. Let's take a look at some surprising examples from Scripture.

Noah, who obeyed and saved humanity and other life, couldn't control his passions, accidentally forming nations that would later be hostile to the ways of God.

Joseph, almost the youngest in a large family of boys and certainly not the most robust, not only was the family pet, to the degradation of relationships, but lacked a certain discreteness in announcing his dreams.

Moses, intelligent but hot-headed, had to hide in the desert for 40 years because of his indiscretion. When finally called out to do his work, he had to have the help of his brother because he stuttered too much to talk to kings. Do you suppose this made Israel reluctant to follow him?

Gideon, after 40 years of Midianite suppression of Israel, has discovered how to fool them. Rather than sift his wheat on the threshing floor at the top of the hill where they can see and steal, he is doing his work in the wine press away from eyes and wind. The work is much harder without wind. Imagine the huffing and puffing.

Suddenly he is visited by God and informed that he, as a mighty man of valor would set Israel free. Gideon protests, "I am the lowest member of my family and my family is the lowest family in our tribe."

I can hear God saying, "You're my man. I am bottom fishing."

How is that for a client? Further, Gideon, after an initial obedience, suffers deep doubt and invents a new method of checking on God that we call "fleeces." Then, when the call to arms produces only 32,000 men aligned against 120,000 Midianites, God instructs Gideon to use a rather silly method that reduces his men to only 300; and they, I believe, were the ones too fat and too crippled to get down on all fours to drink. At least they would give God the glory for the victory. Such clients!

Samson! What a strange character. Mortally vulnerable to the lust of this flesh. Strangely lacking in logical thinking. What did he look like? Not like the Hollywood Arbold Juggernaut version. Were that so, Delilah, his wife, would not have had to ask the source of his strength. More likely he was short, fat and wore suspenders! (personal joke here) Such a client.

David was certainly not the favorite of his family. I sometimes wonder what it was about him that made David such an embarrassment to his father. But after all the sons who were handsome and stately men were seen and rejected, he got the kingly anointing.

Solomon, at his elevation, protests that he is but a child.

The Jewish nation. Chosen because they were so nice and lovable? Hardly. Repeatedly, God calls them stiffnecked and hard of heart. They were not a people, but God made them his people.

Mary. Elevated by some people to almost co-redeemer. Perhaps they missed what I see in Scripture. Mary was blessed (all who know God are blessed), but this means she was the recipient, not the blessor. Nothing about the statement of the angel indicates that she was deserving (none are). Most scholars believe she was about 15 years old. If you have a 15-year-old, can you imagine what it would mean to be the "mother of God"? We expect her to be impervious to the seduction of power. I think we are wrong. Probably, from the evidence I see, Mary was seriously and negatively affected by her new power. She became a pushy mom.

Listen to this attack when Jesus was 12 years old and had remained at the temple: *And when they saw Him, they were astonished; and His mother said to Him, "Son, why have You treated us this way? Behold, your father and I have been anxiously looking for you."* (Luke 2:48 NAS) What are the implications of addressing Jesus this way if she understood who he was?

At the first recorded miracle Jesus turned water into wine, but not before rebuking his mother for being so pushy. Every explanation I have heard does a song and dance to avoid what really happened. Also, the last recorded words of Mary are at that incident. She told the servants to do whatever Jesus told them to do. Wise words there. Had Mary been what some, unfortunately, claim her to be, the New Testament would have been filled with consultation and quotes from her. It is painfully silent. Perhaps she had actually become something of a bother to the early church.

As if that were not enough, Mark 3 informs us that she thought Jesus had lost his mind and she and his brothers had come to take him home. Can you understand with me what the implications are? She thinks she can take the messiah home and get him well! This is a Mary who does not understand. We have not adequately dealt with this amazing incident.

By the way, where is Joseph, now? Why didn't he come to help take Jesus home? Most people assume that he died. Surely some note would have been made of that in Scripture. More likely, having suffered the pain of Mary's pushiness and seeing now that Jesus had it made, decided it was all he could take so he split. The very silence of Scripture lends such evidence. (We are most silent about the most embarrassing.)

Jesus deflects an early attempt to honor Mary. *As Jesus was saying these things, a woman in the crowd called out, "Blessed is the mother who gave you birth and nursed you." He replied, "Blessed rather are those who hear the word of God and obey it."* (Luke 11:27-28)

If Mary was destined to become the road of access to Jesus, as some believe, surely Jesus would have venerated her more at that time.

From the agony of the cross, Jesus gave Mary to John for his safekeeping. Why John? Simple. John had a pushy mother, too, and would know how to properly relate to her.

Finally, Scripture records that Mary joined the 120 on the Day of Pentecost. Apparently, she, too, needed the baptism of the Holy Spirit.

So, when, in the beginning of the New Testament story, Mary describes herself as being of "low estate" she described herself well and thus placed herself in the category of those God uses.

Paul sees this clearly and sums it up for us in ways we tend to ignore in 1 Corinthians 1: 26-29.

Brothers, think of what you were when you were called. Not many of you were wise by human standards; not many were influential; not many were of noble birth. But God chose the foolish things of the world to shame the wise; God chose the weak things of the world to shame the strong. He chose the lowly things of this world and the despised things—and the things that are not— to nullify the things that are, so that no one may boast before him.

That's us folks. God's clients and therefore the clients of the servant. The weak and foolish. That is worth a party.

Authority

Where does authority fit in the servanthood lifestyle? Jesus gave some insight when he confronted the leadership style in the "kingdom of the world."

The Kingdom of the World

> The kings of the Gentiles lord it over them; and those who exercise authority over them call themselves Benefactors. But you are not to be like that. (Luke 22:25-26. See also Mark 10:42,43 and Matthew 20:25,26.)

The implications of this statement are somewhat astounding. Jesus made it clear that his kingdom was not of this world and inferred that his subjects would not use "worldly" methods to protect or enlarge when he told Pilate that if his kingdom were of this world, his subjects would fight—the normal worldly method of settling disputes.

But fighting is not the only worldly method available to us for kingdom use. Just as Jesus was greatest in his kingdom and his servanthood was the pattern for operation within his kingdom laws, so the world has its kingdom and a pattern of operation. The normal gentile-worldly system was readily apparent to the observer. Jesus did not need to tell them that Gentile leaders (or greatest in the world kingdom) would lord it over others, exercise authority over them and liked to be given titles such as "Benefactor."

My natural reaction is to say, "But how else can you deal with people? This is a different world now and people are like dumb sheep who have to be told what to do." So, because of an approach to leadership that says "If it works in managing people, it must be good," I (we in the church) have somewhat unquestioningly adopted worldly systems of pyramidal hierarchy that, if one were to examine us, would be no different from any profit-making corporation.

The whole question of authority and how to use it in the church continues to be a hot one for committed Christians with theologically sound systems varying greatly. If I may freely paraphrase Robert Burns, the Scottish poet: "If only God would give us the power to see ourselves as others see us." I get so lost in the acceptance of "things as they are" that I cannot see the subtle ways that I lord it over others or exercise authority over others. Likewise, because it seems such a logical flow in the world, I readily adopt titles and other forms that will quickly let the world know my status.

Sometimes I ponder the possibility of asking someone who doesn't understand either church or world (a child, maybe?) to examine my working sphere and tell me in what ways it would be evident to the outsider that I am the "boss" without their ever having had interaction with me.

A few years ago in a newspaper-type publication, a minister discussed the question of "What shall we let laymen call us?" After saying the things to be expected such as "Being a minister is a high calling," and "People need to learn to respect the office of preacher, pastor, etc.", he concluded in his article that it was not appropriate for people to call a minister by his (her) first name. He felt that although "Reverend" was acceptable, the barest minimum must be to use the word "Pastor" before whatever name we permitted them to use.

Now, I find that whole discussion distasteful and especially that conclusion. It sounds suspiciously like the argument of the disciples over who was greatest. However, I must admit that this has not always been so with me. The whole process of "entering the ministry" has with it the question of when it actually occurs. A questionnaire given to me during college days asked among other things, "At what point did you begin to see yourself as a 'Reverend'?"

Once, that was an important question to me, and I recall the feeling of power that went with my first set of printed bank checks that had the title "Reverend" before my name. It was as if my identity was now complete. Others may be called "Doctor" or

"Your Honor" or "Counselor" but now I was right up there with them in professional recognition (in my eyes) by bearing such a title.

Now, I am embarrassed by how I acted and embarrassed by the whole struggle to gain our status in the world as a recognized profession. It seems almost bad enough to be arguing over who is greatest in the kingdom of God without also going into the world and arguing with them in their territory over who is greatest overall.

Either arrogantly or with inner distress, I automatically examine any structure, any institution that uses the name of our Lord, to see if it is organized along kingdom principles or whether it has the pyramid and titles of corporation or world government. I don't even need to detail for you how disillusioning those observations have been.

Being a pastor has forced me to struggle with common questions. How can you get things done without the efficiency of the world system? Must we be the laughing stock of those who see our missed organizational opportunities? If we are going to do big things in a big world, how can we avoid these minimal world structure systems?

I do not know the answers to these questions, and the answers that I "suspect" might be true are too radical to freely speak. Perhaps faith in God also includes faith that kingdom principles will work in our institutional lives as well as in our personal lives. Perhaps salvation from our personal sins also means salvation from our corporate sins. Repentance may mean turning from "Gentile" ways personally and institutionally. People in "authority" have often admitted to me that "faith" and what we "had to do" were not necessarily the same.

The Kingdom of the Church

Generally recognized as having been written specifically for the Jews, the Gospel of Matthew contains some statements that we cannot avoid applying to any group that acts in the name of the Lord.

> The teachers of the law and the Pharisees sit in Moses' seat. So you must obey them and do everything they tell you. But do not do what they do, for they do not practice what they preach. They tie up heavy loads and put them on men's shoulders, but they themselves are not willing to lift a finger to move them. Everything they do is done for men to see: they make their phylacteries wide and the tassels of their prayer shawls long; they love the place of honor at banquets and the most important seats in the synagogues; they love to be greeted in the marketplaces and to have men call them "Rabbi." But you are not to be called "Rabbi," for you have only one Master and you are all brothers. And do not call any-

one on earth "Father," for you have one Father, and he is in heaven. Nor are you to be called "Teacher," for you have one Teacher, the Christ. (Matthew 23:2-10)

Apparently, the kingdom of the church operates with little difference from that of the world. The description in the Scripture above is remarkably like that given of the Gentile leaders. The simplest message in the Scripture quoted is that we must practice what we preach (be an example) and not do anything that establishes for us a higher status than our brothers.

Most of the comments on that Scripture tend to use Jesus' statements to attack the Catholic priests permitting themselves to be called "Father," while conveniently ignoring any particular application to ourselves. However, as stated earlier, I find myself using status symbols rather readily and often requiring of my parishioners sacrifices that I have not exampled.

How long does it take before any revival movement begins to take on the looks of establishment and ritual replaces spontaneity and relationship. In a Beetle Bailey cartoon, General Halftrack finds himself in a contemplative mood and goes for a walk with his hands folded behind his back and his head bent staring at the ground as he walks along. He returns to his office and muses, "It is good to get out, walk and think once in a while like that." So, he calls his secretary to take a memo and in the final frame you see the entire army camp marching to their new orders, in file, with their hands clasped behind their backs and their heads bent over staring at the ground as they walk.

These are the sorts of things that happen when authority replaces relationship and roles become institutionalized. These methods are highly natural for human beings, and for that reason create anxiety in me when I am forced to think of all the implications. The free-flowing roles and growth of revivals seem to stand in opposition to the formation of institutional authorities, yet such freedom leaves many people uncomfortable and we end up as prisoners of history building cathedrals destined to lie empty. The implications cannot be escaped.

It would be difficult for a servant, whether Pharisee or Gentile to say to his master, "I am your servant and you will do what I tell you." But our carnal natures have us establishing a pecking order within ten years of the beginning of cult or cathedral.

If you have ever observed a flock of chickens, you know that within days of the gathering of the flock a pecking order develops. There will be one chicken that no other chicken will dare peck, yet he will and does peck every other chicken in the barnyard. Then there will be a "number two" chicken who pecks everyone except the "number one" chicken and that chicken is the only one who will peck him and on down the row until finally there is one chicken at the bottom who pecks no other chicken and every chicken in the yard will peck him. Usually he has no tail feathers as a result and may not survive. Chickens are much too human or vice versa.

Surely there are no rationalizations left to us for self-aggrandizement and self-elevation if we are followers of Jesus and see ourselves as slaves.

The Kingdom of God

The scriptures quoted above from Luke 22 and Matthew 23 are direct confrontations of Jesus with the kingdoms of the world and the church. In each of those sections, he contrasts them with the operating system of his own kingdom. Let us see the contrast:

> The greatest among you will be your servant. For whoever exalts himself will be humbled, and whoever humbles himself will be exalted. (Matthew 23:11,12)

> But you are not to be like that. Instead, the greatest among you should be like the youngest, and the one who rules like the one who serves. (Luke 22:26)

So, it appears that the single thing that marks the contrast of the subjects of Jesus and those caught in the systems of the world is that of servanthood. The reigning question is whether we will live for ourselves or for others.

If there are overriding practical lessons we can gain from the consideration of these contrasting kingdoms, they seem to be these:

1. Avoid titles and clothing or other public displays that establish our superiority over others or a special higher spiritual status.

2. Do not *lord it over others* or put ourselves in the place of being someone else's master.

3. Whatever we expect others to do, we should be the example.

Fundraising

America "the rich" plays in the minds of most Developing Countries and causes them to want to come here even as they hate us at the same time. One friend of mine who came over from Africa actually thought that when you arrive in America, they give you money. Imagine his disappointment.

Often, when friends from foreign countries visited me, I honored their requests and took them to the churches and religious centers to see for themselves what they had heard about in their own country. Without fail, they were deeply disappointed. I had to explain to them that this is an advertising country and, especially in religious advertising, candor is only a distant rumor.

My friends also wanted to see "Christian television." I accommodated them. They puzzled constantly over the fundraising techniques. You would think, from observation, that God is broke."Why do they spend so much time taking up money?" "Are times that hard?" "They could never do this in our country," were terms I frequently heard. As much as I could, I explained that television is a hungry medium and is truly costly, but at the same time, few, if any, of these money-raisers are accountable for the money they raise. Many of them live with the exceedingly rich.

Schools of thought differ over money. Should we pay as we go on church buildings or borrow to get them up fast so the congregation can grow? Should we seek funds or simply live within the means we have? How much fundraising is enough? I want to give an answer to these questions, but first let me tell you a true story of the pitfalls of needing to "raise" money.

A new Christian funding organization invited a number of churches and non-profit organizations to allow their system to raise funds for them. The guidelines were simple—deposit a certain amount of money and we will double it in six months or so (from secret donors). If this sounds like a classic Ponzi scheme, that is exactly what it turned out to be. Some did get their money doubled, but in the end, most lost—grandly—millions of dollars. I noticed that the people who lost were those who, by reason of policy or polity, were willing to use whatever means available to raise funds. Apparently, none of those who lost money were of the "live on what you have" school.

Now, in the business world, you have to spend money to make money. What rules guide the Christian? Would "seek first the kingdom" be a valid philosophy? Numerous companies exist to help organizations convince the public to contribute funds, but how do we learn to seek first the kingdom? Do any organizations exist to teach that as the principal source of funding?

Now, let's answer some of the earlier questions. Should we borrow to build buildings? First, buildings should not be built speculatively, not with the "If you build it, they will come" type of philosophy. If a congregation must be taxed and tapped constantly to meet the payments, the plan to build was a mistake. If the size of the congregation dictates and payments would be a snap, borrowing might be appropriate.

So, how much fundraising is enough? That which is merely biblical. The only fundraising I see in the New Testament is when Paul apparently collected for the needs of the believers in Jerusalem who were under great persecution. It doesn't seem that he even took out a percentage for "overhead."

Somewhere in all of this, we must trust the Holy Spirit to take the Scripture on the subject of giving and manifest it in our hearts as generosity. If that doesn't meet the need, we must decide that the need is not actually there.

The best control I have found is never to attempt to raise funds. In fact, the best method is to resist even the mention of money outside the normal marching through the Word in teaching. That way, whatever happens, you will know was the work of God.

Freedom

The mere subject of taxes raises blood pressures and brings out the fighting instinct. Sometime in May, the US Government announces a "tax freedom" day. After this date, you work for yourself and your income no longer simply pays taxes. Freedom.

Less than two months later, we celebrate the Declaration of Independence of our country when we declared that everyone had the right to "life, liberty and the pursuit of happiness." We have fought wars to guarantee or protect our freedom. Freedom is important enough for us to mark, celebrate and fight. A famous bell rang to signal the decree. We call it the "Liberty Bell."

But a crack appears in the bell. Not everyone in this land lives free. Bondage takes forms far beyond the oppression of a foreign government or the collections of a local government. The strongest prisons have no fences, bars or addresses. Even in this, the freest of countries, mankind's self-centeredness holds him in the cruelest of jails. The jail of flesh laughs at attempts to escape. Government programs designed to free people from deadly addictions are miserable failures, not even exceeding the rate of natural recovery.

Addiction and Greed

The jails of addiction are jails of selfishness. No one ever enters their doors for the sake of others. One can never say, "I am a drunkard, or drug addict for your benefit." Self is the culprit. However bad drugs and alcohol may be, they are minor leaguers compared to other jails for which there are no government programs.

No bars are as thick as the bars of greed behind which the wealthy are held. Escape from those bars is about as easy as pushing a camel through the eye of a needle. A man with a billion can do far more damage to mankind than a man with a gun or a drink. A famous old saying is "A man with a briefcase can steal far more than a man with a gun." Yet, you never hear of any of the world's richest people begging for relief from their greed or asking for entry into a richness recovery program. So self is the cruelest of jailers.

I once had a rich friend. One day, after he heard me speak about the subject of greed, he and his wife reported to me that they had just lost all their money and would have to move away to much lesser surroundings. He admitted that it was simply greed that caused them to lose. I appreciated the candor of my friend. They had thrown all caution to the wind and had been captured in a scam. Their high living came to an end.

If one achieves the fullness of wealth and power in his fleshly striving, what would the ultimate be? Surely a sense of rest and fulfillment, but no, history proves the opposite. Solomon had the ultimate in material goods and fleshly delights but still called it all vanity. Nebuchadnezzar had it all but couldn't control his rage over someone failing to worship a gold statue. Alexander conquered the world and cried because there were no more worlds to conquer. Is there any hope?

OK, Tell Me the Truth

Occasionally, libraries will have engraved in marble above their door, "The Truth Shall Set You Free." This, of course, comes from the mouth of Jesus; however, if you approach the librarian, "OK, tell me the Truth," you will be considered something of a nut case to one whose life is surrounded by fiction and nonfiction. The world sees truth as a gathering of facts. Unfortunately, they have to keep redefining facts.

For a moment, let's look at this often misunderstood biblical principle of "Truth setting you free." I take the liberty to condense and paraphrase John 8:31-36:

1. If you believe in me,
2. And follow my teachings,
3. Then you are my disciples (learners).

4. Then you shall know the Truth and the Truth shall set you free.

5. If Jesus makes you free, you are truly free.

Anything less only produces a freedom to be in bondage. Anything less leaves our greatest jailer still in charge—self. Is it any wonder that Jesus would state clearly, *It is the Spirit who gives life; the flesh profits nothing. The words that I speak to you are spirit, and they are life.* (John 6:63 NAS)

Is it any wonder that, once the disciples realized that he was the Messiah, Jesus could now offer the highest freedom: *If anyone desire to come after me, let him deny himself, and take up his cross and follow me. For whoever desires to save his life will lose it, but whoever loses his life for my sake will find it.* (Matthew 16:24-25 NKJ)

So, my cross is this constant desire of my flesh to revert to bondage. So many things provide my flesh pleasure that it rarely manages to count the price being charged. I heard of one farmer at a county fair who was urged by a hawker to try a new food. The farmer replied, "No. I've got enough wants I can't satisfy now." He was wise.

Though in danger of violating the very principle I am presenting, the question remains, "What is the payoff for accepting this freedom from the flesh—boredom?" Quite the contrary. First, I am issued rest. No longer do I have to spend what should be productive time merely satisfying the flesh. Second, I finally find life. We all want to find our lives.

That is why we are greedy and selfish. However, he who made us also knows how his product works. He who made us told us that to find our lives we must give them away.

I call that a "published secret." You can plaster that message on billboards all over the world and people will still not know. Why? Because spiritual truths cannot be discerned by our flesh. So, if one wants freedom of country, he can fight for it, and thank God for those who have. But bondage will remain until we are free from ourselves.

Whose Will?

Some stalwarts wish to obtain that self-freedom by will power. They shut themselves away from the world, or deny themselves some thing as if that provides freedom or fulfills the invitation of Jesus to denial. Or whole religious systems are developed to attempt to reach a stability where one wants or needs only moderation. However, it doesn't work. One man's moderation is another man's excess. Even the billionaires will define themselves as moderate. Part of our great bondage is self-deception. That is why Jesus said to deny our self.

Paul the Apostle gives a scary review of freedom that seems to deny all that I have said to you so far. Listen to his remarkable statement: *All things are lawful for me,....* (1 Corinthians 6:12 NKJ) Have you ever heard a more brazen, anarchistic statement? It sounds like he has taken his freedom much too far.

But don't jump too quickly to a conclusion. Notice the limits he puts on this freedom: ...*but all things are not helpful. All things are lawful for me, but I will not be brought under the power of any.* (1 Corinthians 6:12 NKJ)

Obviously Paul understands the nature of Jesus. Freedom means release from the bondage of ourselves and our relentless fleshliness. Just like Jesus, freedom means living for others, not the freedom to display our freedom. Freedom means walking clean. No wonder Jesus said to *deny ourselves*.

So where do we go? Back to Jesus! No true freedom exists before him or without him. Somebody has to save us. We cannot save ourselves. We are miserable, selfish, greedy worms until we find and believe in the great others-centered one. With him, it's a wonderful life.

Forgiveness

Jesus changed "eye for eye" to "forgive." Until then, humanity left all the forgiving to God. A simple study of the nature of God proves that he forgave all manner of sin. (Exodus 34:6) Now, with Jesus moving the Law to a spiritual plane, those who follow God must also forgive. Jesus relayed to us that masterpiece of communication with God we call "The Lord's Prayer." (Matthew 6:9-13 KJ) The centerpiece of the prayer is *And forgive us our debts, as we forgive our debtors.* Only that portion does Jesus choose to elaborate.

Jesus informs us that if we do not forgive those who sin against us, neither will the Father forgive our sins. This is an awesome and scary statement. Forgiveness so anchors the nature of God that if we expect to walk with him, we must, at minimum, practice the trait that is at the core. No longer an option, now a requirement, forgiveness soars to the highest level of Christian living. Its effects are too broad to ignore.

Perfect Example

God's example of forgiveness has been with us a long time. We can never say that we cannot forgive because we don't know how. Centuries of God's faithfulness have shown us precisely how to forgive. With Jesus we see the forgiveness of God with skin wrapped around it. Jesus stated that all manner of sin against him would be forgiven. (Matthew 12:31)

Peter, chafing under the requirement to forgive in the prayer of Jesus, apparently thought as rabbinically as he could until finally (after some time) felt that he had discovered the loophole. So, bringing up this question of forgiveness with Jesus in Matthew 18 (12 chapters later) Peter asked how often he should forgive someone who sinned against him. He offered his own generous response—seven times. Surely Peter expected Jesus to compliment him for such generosity. However, Jesus moved forgiveness into a whole new plane by stating that Peter should forgive seventy times seven.

I don't think Jesus was limiting forgiveness to 490 times a day, although that would be hardly possible, but was saying that forgiveness was simply a way of life, not a mathematical formula. It is impossible for someone to sin against us 490 times in one day then seek and receive forgiveness 490 times.

Maybe Jesus was telling us that our heart for forgiving should exceed someone's ability to sin against us.

Perfect Clarity

Just so the slow-learning Peter (and we latecomers) would understand perfectly, Jesus offers a parable following the forgiveness question.

"Therefore, the kingdom of heaven is like a king who wanted to settle accounts with his servants. As he began the settlement, a man who owed him ten thousand talents was brought to him. Since he was not able to pay, the master ordered that he and his wife and his children and all that he had be sold to repay the debt.

"The servant fell on his knees before him. 'Be patient with me,' he begged, 'and I will pay back everything.' The servant's master took pity on him, canceled the debt and let him go.

"But when that servant went out, he found one of his fellow servants who owed him a hundred denarii. He grabbed him and began to choke him. 'Pay back what you owe me!' he demanded.

"His fellow servant fell to his knees and begged him, 'Be patient with me, and I will pay you back.'

"But he refused. Instead, he went off and had the man thrown into prison until he could pay the debt.

"When the other servants saw what had happened, they were greatly distressed and went and told their master everything that had happened.

"Then the master called the servant in. 'You wicked servant,' he said, 'I canceled all that debt of yours because you begged me to. Shouldn't you have had mercy on your fellow servant just as I had on you?' In anger his master turned him over to the jailers to be tortured, until he should pay back all he owed. (Matthew 18:23-34)

Jesus comments simply and powerfully on this incredible story by saying: *This is how my heavenly Father will treat each of you unless you forgive your brother from your heart.* (Matthew 18:35) The reality and symbolism are unforgettable.

Perfect Health

This brings me to a belief that has grown in my heart through the years as I have seen the debate over how we produce health in people, especially what we call "mental health." I am convinced that forgiveness is the secret to wholeness of spirit and soul. Consequently, it seems to me "The Lord's Prayer" when prayed with understanding restores or improves man's relationship with God and with his world.

A key buzzword is "victimization." Criminals often plead innocence claiming they merely respond to a bad early life. In other words, "I'm not guilty of making you a victim, since I'm just a victim." Others harbor resentment and bitterness that destroy relationships and disease personalities. They would claim that they are only the victims of the evil actions of other people.

However, let me set forth a belief that I find totally scriptural: No one who forgives can ever be a victim. The man who forgives frees himself completely from the bondage of anyone's past action toward him. Do you realize how many wars would not happen if forgiveness existed in the hearts of people? Do you realize how healthy the forgiver becomes? Do you realize how much mind and spirit time is released for profitable use whenever someone releases bitterness and resentment to a spirit of forgiveness?

Forgiveness is not only a way of doing what is right and best for others, but it is the finest possible thing we can do for ourselves. Nothing, I repeat nothing, profits from unforgiveness. Yet we hang on to our grievances as if forgiving were an indication of weakness. The fact is, only those who know the creator and choose to be strong in him can forgive.

Until we understood germs, the unwashed hands of a surgeon guaranteed death for half of his patients. Unforgiveness on our part is like having unwashed hands in our ministry to others. We only spread disease. The forgiveness of God is either funneled through us to others or else shielded from our own reception by our unforgiveness. Forgiveness cannot be bottled.

If we funnel forgiveness through, it cleans us and gives us health and provides clean hands for us to heal others. Forgiveness also frees a person to receive the benefits of the other great health producer of Scripture. Jesus said that if we want to find our lives (be whole), we must lose them.

Unless we are free from the bondage of bitterness, we cannot give attention to losing our lives. Because of the destructive results of unforgiveness (preventing God's forgiveness of us), some people believe that unforgiveness is the *sin unto death* of 1 John 5:16 (KJ).

If firmness is required in a relationship, forgive first or else we suffer from the sin of anger. If discipline is required, forgive first, so that the action will be redemptive rather than merely retributive.

Perfect Finale

When Jesus hung on the cross, there remained one possibility for sin that would have nullified his sacrifice. Jesus could have responded to this miserable mocking crowd with anger and vengeance, but he didn't. Instead, his first words on the cross swept clear all possible final sin, *Father forgive them, they do not know what they are doing.* (Luke 23:34) Jesus, nailed to the cross, was the freest person of all.

Jesus could have ended his mission in perfect misery, but he chose the path of his Father. As in the story of the unforgiving servant, the finale was to be turned over to the torturers until he paid the last penny. How powerfully symbolic.

Even passing observation reveals that unforgiving people live tortured lives. Payment for such debt remains beyond our means. Tortured people cannot pay. They only go further into debt. Only one door remains for freedom from torture—forgiveness.

Perfect Love

To the degree we sense our own forgiveness, we offer the same to others. If, from our own pride, we feel that our sins are minimal and we did God more of a favor to come to him than he did in forgiving us, then we will treat others with a harshness ungodly in itself. In Luke 7, Jesus spoke very plainly to a Pharisee named Simon that whomever is forgiven little loves little and whomever is forgiven much loves much.

Simon must have been stung in the presence of the "much sinning" woman who obviously loved more because she knew the truth about her own sinfulness. Simon denied the truth about himself, thus felt little to forgive and offered no forgiveness to others. Perhaps, when we see a harsh and unforgiving person, we also see a proud and arrogant person. Humility causes us to see the truth about ourselves and drives us to our knees in repentance.

Perfect Prayer

God wants to hear from and speak to his children, so prayer is far more powerful than any natural force known to man. Nuclear bombs pale at the power of prayer. One simple thing blocks this awesome power: unforgiveness. Jesus clearly stated, *And when ye stand praying, forgive, if ye have ought against any: that your Father also which is in heaven may forgive you your trespasses.* (Mark 11:25 KJ)

God is not impressed with our repetition or intensity in prayer and certainly not in our traditions or positions of prayer. However, the position of the heart—kneeling, forgiving—opens the door of heaven in many ways. Proper praying calls for the very best for our enemies—the kind of prayer we would want prayed for us.

Perfect Contrast

The output of stage and screen bears fault for immorality, violence and greed. (You can also substitute the word "government" for "stage and screen.") But one largely overlooked ungodliness is the bent for vengeance rather than justice or forgiveness. Few writers seek to achieve justice for justice sake. Justice, you see, ultimately rests on the belief that some things are simply right and some things are simply wrong. Since God alone offers such a firm moral position, and God is foreign to the sinful heart, the only acceptable position for secular consumption is vengeance.

Heros are no longer heros because they fought for what was right. They are heros simply because they won by gaining vengeance. Society applauds that and fills theaters to affirm its approval. Politics reveals its heart in one of its laws of operation. "Don't get mad, get even!"

The forgiveness of Jesus stands in perfect contrast to the world view. However, some great writers have been touched by the master forgiver. At the urging of a dear friend in Chicago, my wife and I went to the stage production of "les Miserables" by Victor Hugo when it came to our town. This powerful story of the converting effect of forgiveness and grace upon a person so moved us. When it was over, we waited for the crowd to leave so I would not be embarrassed for letting them see this foolish old man crying.

So?

So, as the days grow short to the end of history, our way of living becomes more valuable. Paul in

Colossians 3 says: *Forgive, just as the Father forgave you...and wrap all of this with love.* (my paraphrase) His forgiveness was not less than 100% and contained no prerequisites. Clear enough!

Worship
In Spirit and Truth

Back in the 1970s, along with the revival God was giving us, there came a refreshing, creative surge of new forms of worship. Until that time, by my observation, worship seemed to fall into two camps—wild or dead. Both were impersonal.

That surge touched my parched being in two ways, almost simultaneously. One was the rediscovered art of singing the Scripture. I played the records of those first Scripture songs time and time again, often simply lying down between the speakers of my rudimentary stereo to let my being absorb the words and music. It was an acre of Heaven.

The second touch of the surge was a wave of new worship that accompanied the revival. I was still "back East," as Californians would say, when records of entirely new songs passed into my hands by divine coincidence. My cultural rigidities were shaken enough to crack open and let joy explode. A new river had to be penned in on my map.

Gentleness marked this new wave of worship along with naturalness and intimacy. Although this worship springing from the hearts of the Jesus Movement was intense, gentleness kept it from having any frightening forms. With the simplest of instruments, the guitar, a leader would simply begin to worship—no barking orders or cajoling. The knowledge that nothing would be done to embarrass you or single you out in an audience offered a delightful new freedom to worship. The neophyte and the sophisticate were equally at home.

Refreshingly, worship was no longer a three-song-and-offering preliminary for a sermon. Now, it was an entity of its own—a joyful companion to the receiving of the Word. Songs that could be easily remembered and sung brought the choirs down from their lofts and made music the property of everyone. Now it was "natural" to sing and play these new songs repeatedly all day on our new technological tape-wonders. No clever methods were needed to urge the overflow of our hearts past our vocal cords. Though we were gladly together, we were still locked into privacy with God as we sang personally to him of our love. We learned to linger with God. The lingering continues.

Power flowed from this rediscovery of worship, and over the years, power in excess. Just as a river will form dangerous whirlpools at the edges, so the power of worship has swirled in some problems around the edges. I wish to address those problems in hopes that we can keep the channel of praise flowing.

Creeping Problems

Worshiping Worship

The first problem that demands attention is one that is typical of any powerful expression of God that spawns a movement—in time we begin to focus on the movement rather than on God. The "Faith" movement became one that exhibited faith in faith. Now I detect in what might be called a "Worship" movement a tendency to worship worship. When I hear sermons and read writings that go to great lengths to show me what worship has done in the past and how powerful worship was in Scripture, then I realize that the focus has become on worship rather than on the God of worship; and a certain amount of worship by formula has developed.

A typical result of the "worship of worship" is energy spent developing new and creative forms of worship because worship is so powerful rather than focusing on God himself and exploring the release of all our attention toward him. The distinction may be subtle sometimes, but it is there.

Sometimes, the fact that God told Israel to send Judah (Judah means "praise") into battle first causes us to think that this was some generic statement about praise in all its forms. Those who hold to this theory as the primary means of battling Satan forget the fact that it was also Judah (Judas) who betrayed Jesus.

Sewing Up the Veil

A second problem has been born from the womb of an inaccurate view of all that Jesus came to do. Frequently, I meet the teaching that in order to worship properly, we must adopt a "Davidic" form. This system includes copying worship methods that can be seen or deduced from the life of David and in the Psalms as well as approaching God and worship in progressive stages as if moving through the rooms or places of the Temple until finally you emotionally or spiritually reach the Holy of Holies.

The "Davidic" forms are rousingly presented and include dance, banner, song and shout as well as other forms I have not observed. The "Temple" approach attempts to attain (primarily by choice of song) progressive intimacy with God until finally, in the most intimate moment with him, one can go behind the veil into the place of the Mercy Seat.

Although I agree with the goal of those who insist on "Davidic" or "Temple" forms and would not question their love of God and worship of him, it still seems to me that with their forms they are attempting to resew the veil that was torn open when Jesus was crucified. By paying the ultimate and final sacrifice, Jesus made it possible for us to ...*come boldly to the throne of grace* (Mercy Seat) ...*and find grace to help in time of need.* (Hebrews 4:16 NKJ) Indeed, the Glory of God left the Holy of Holies when the veil was ripped, as Jesus indicated when he said their house was left *desolate.* When I am worshiping with those who feel we must march through the Temple,

I feel a little sadness for them; because, while they think they are still in the outer court, I and they are actually instantly in the Holy of Holies.

In Spirit and in Truth

My greatest argument against adherence to any system comes from the words of Jesus to the Samaritan woman at the well. Jesus informed her that *...a time is coming when you will worship the Father neither on this mountain nor in Jerusalem. ...true worshipers will worship the Father in spirit and truth, for they are the kind of worshipers the Father seeks.* (John 4:21,23) At this point, Jesus was laying aside all formulas and places as a prerequisite for true worship. The Temple is now our hearts. Worship is anywhere and any time and in whatever form focuses adoration on God. Any attempt to return to a form associated with the Temple or to any form as a prerequisite is a violation of these words of Jesus. In my observation, those forms focus my attention on the forms and the worshipers rather than on God.

Neither worshiping worship by the intensity of our attention to worship itself nor dependence on some form as a necessity are insurmountable problems, but they are problems, nonetheless. Unfortunately, worshiping worship or developing formulas produces deviations in worship leaders that must be brought back on course and develops a guilt and anxiety among worshipers from which they must be freed.

The Worship Leader Mystique

Since worship has grown beyond the "mere preliminary" label in a service and now stands on its own, the task of being a worship leader also takes on new meaning. In my past experience, the worship leader was most valued for his ability to exhort, cajole and, hopefully, involve the congregation in energetic singing and other forms of worship expression. Since worship has taken on renewed interest, there is less need for external pushing. Now, the leader's own musical skills and the example of worship become the desired traits. Also, the worship leader takes on a much more important role; because, now, worship typically lasts longer.

However, the new longer role of the leader creates a certain territoriality that has brought division in more than one church I know. Whenever the worship leader begins to feel that the worship service belongs to him and that his worship understanding surpasses that of the pastor, trouble has arisen that will usually mean the exit of the worship leader.

The Effective Worship Leader

Cooperation

An effective worship leader realizes that he is an extended hand of the pastor and that the pastor is actually the worship leader. The worship leader must never assume that he is more in touch with the action of the Holy Spirit than the pastor. God has placed the pastor in responsibility and the worship leader must never subvert that position. The worship leader must never feel that worship is incomplete if the pastor signals a time to end. To oppose the pastor's discernment is an arrogance that can only destroy the worship leader's effectiveness.

Occasionally, I see worship leaders who feel they are in charge of the theology of the church and attempt to bring in their own set of teachings through their worship. Sometimes they succeed in supplanting church theology because they are popular and effective. When they do this, they have sacrificed their servanthood and sewn the seeds of division.

Invisibility

The good leader knows that his job is to become invisible. He is merely a bridge carrying the attention of the people to God, and anything that interrupts that attention is a roadblock thrown in their way. Leadership does not mean an opportunity to show off skills or knowledge, only an opportunity to show the face of God.

I once watched a leader stop a congregation twice during a song, because he felt we weren't singing it right. It was a painful time as we bent to his wishes. We finally sang it right, according to him, but he had destroyed the worship moment.

An invisible worship leader will avoid beginning worship with a song people can't sing or try to teach a new song at the very start. To do this makes people aware of their own inadequacy and resentful of the skill of the leader. After a few attempts at something new, a congregation feels defeated and only slowly enters worship. I deeply enjoy having someone pull me quickly into adoration of God with a song readily known and singable (a true "call to worship") and then let learning of a new song be the result of my desire to further worship rather than the need of the leader to teach me a new song.

An invisible leader sees his skills in an humble manner. In worship, I believe music skills are for equipping, not for exhibition. Consequently, the leader should practice his musical abilities in order for him to feel comfortable with his own skills—then he can focus his attention on God and the congregation. Also, his skills, as he improves them, will become so congruous with the worship that he blends with the people rather than interrupts them.

The invisible leader assumes that people came to worship and does not tell them that they should or need to convince them that they can. He beckons and does not shove. He invites, not threatens.

Presence

When I see a good worship leader I notice a difficult-to-define trait about him that I call "presence." This trait is noticeable in that he is fully "there" and given to God and the people and yet not lost in his own thoughts and agenda. Presence has several parts. One, is "resonance." Resonance is the ability to flow with the culture in which you are leading worship. Such a leader would instinctively know not to do a clapping song in a "high church" situation nor sing a funeral dirge at a child's dedication.

A leader with resonance is as aware of the people and their needs as he is of his own music. Consequently, he can think of the need to reduce their anxiety about themselves and what is going on so that they can focus their attention on God. Indeed, the term "resonance" speaks of helping people be in communication with God.

Another facet of "presence" is "tongue control." The leader must suppress anything that would divert a Godward look, including any tendency to focus on the leader because of his voice. Whenever the leader decides to do any talking, he should consider every word to be a flat tire. Comments, explanations, exhortations from the worship leader wrestle my attention away from God himself. Nothing is more disconcerting that to begin worship, fix my attention on God, and then have the worship leader stop and encourage me to worship or berate me for not having done it well enough. Exhortation from a leader to worship better merely focuses my attention on what I am doing, not on God himself.

One need not even say, "Let's sing this next song in worship to God." Of course we will! What is the purpose of the meeting, anyway? Or one need not say, "Sing this next song as a prayer." If it is a prayer, it will be self-evident and the words of exhortation only insult our intelligence. A worship leader need not master the obvious.

Another part of "presence" is "anxiety-reduction." The leader is alert to disruptions of worship beside mere talk. With some frequency, I find worship leaders demanding that I turn and stare at someone else as I sing a certain song such as "I Love You with the Love of the Lord." Nothing sends my anxiety level higher and wrenches my attention from God more than that. When I see this happen, I assume the leader has his own agenda and does not understand what problem he has created in the congregation.

One item of congregational action that has all the elements of excellence but can still fall into the category of anxiety/distraction is for the leader to ask that everyone hold the hands of the persons on either side. Here is the potential problem: Though there is a command to take the hand of the person next to you, there is not a comfortable opposite command. When we are told to stand up, there is a comfortable opposite—"you may be seated." Not so with holding hands. What would you say? "Unhand each other?" So, if a leader plans to have us hold hands, he must think ahead and be sure that there is a natural moment soon when we can free each other from our sweaty palms.

Perhaps the most common disruption is the practice of standing during the entire worship service. This is obviously easier for a young and muscular group. Many people who are unable to stand that long would feel themselves to be outside of the realm of acceptance. After the first 15 minutes I begin to notice my feet and legs more than I am noticing the opportunity to worship. Also, because I have to stand for another hour to speak I don't want to tire too early.

Also counterproductive is excessive movement, standing and then sitting, for instance. It is not distracting to me to stand at a certain point in worship or when it truly seems appropriate; but, when it is popcorn up and down, I begin to wonder if the leader is nervous. Also, I find that "presence" lacking when a leader has us stand at a certain point and I never can figure out why he did, or to tell us all to stand and then say we can sit down or stand up depending on what we like. When such an uncertain trumpet sounds, individuals will stand, sometimes by themselves for the whole time. Frankly, it is a distraction. This is not to say that moments of spontaneous standing are out of order, but institutionalized individual standing is. Why is it a distraction? Because it makes others take notice of the person and wonder if he is a "show-off" or else if they are not spiritual enough to stand. Once again, our attention is away from God himself.

If a leader chooses to have people stand, which is fine, he should be aware that there is also a need to tell them to sit down. "Presence" will be alert to the feelings of the congregation, not just to a preset agenda.

Sensitivity

Another somewhat-hard-to-define but you-know-when-you-have-it trait is sensitivity. The sensitive worship leader is one who can freely set the example by his worship but stay constantly alert to the signals of the pastor and the reactions of the congregation.

Often I see worship leaders who have led a successful worship time begin to feel that they are "on a roll" and will push to maintain length and intensity of spirit as far as they can. Often they resent turning the service over to the pastor because they feel that worship is going so well that to stop for some other part of the schedule would be to quench the Spirit. That is an erroneous assumption that comes from a misunderstanding of what he is actually supposed to do. He knows that the important thing is that worship has truly occurred, not that it has gone on for a long time.

Ethics

A good worship leader will have a high sense of ethics in his relationship with the people so that he won't have a hidden agenda or try to "do" something to the people by manipulative methods. He will be careful not to be just a collector of ideas from other worship situations to "try" on the people. He will simply see himself as a servant who happens to have certain skills to lay at the feet of God and the people.

A pastor once asked a question of me, a question frequently heard, "Can you recommend a worship leader who will not split the church?" Stop and think of the implications of that question. Can you answer?

I suppose even worship condenses to a proper understanding of the two greatest commandments that Jesus seemed to feel were only one: *"You shall love the Lord your God with all your heart, with all your soul, and with all your mind. This is the first and great commandment. And the second is like it, You shall love your neighbor as yourself. On these two commandments hang all the Law and the Prophets."* (Matthew 22:37-40 NKJ)

If a leader can help me love God and people and can maintain an honest relationship with the people who follow, the high wave of our new worship should roll on for a long time.

Fear

Fear far exceeds faith in prompting the actions of man. Fear is a favorite and powerful force for the manipulators of this world. No one escapes its bondage. If you want an interesting insight into your own soul, get a group of children talking about what they fear.

I can recall a myriad of fears, mostly unfounded, in my childhood that kept me from many of the joys I should have had. Overhearing the talk of my parents during World War II, my greatest fear was that they might take my father away in the draft. I had no idea what the "draft" was, but I knew that it made people disappear.

I loved the small forest behind our house and the creek that ran through it; however, it became off-limits to me because a kid six years older than I threatened me. He said he could press a spot on his arm cast and send snakes running to get me if I wandered again into his private domain. Lacking the knowledge to scoff at this statement, I floundered in the irrational world that feeds the fears of childhood. I remember that event as I think of the territorial threats and wars that engulf commerce and nations.

Some valid, usable fears, well founded, also shaped my life. I feared the street. The trucks and cars that whizzed by were obviously larger than I. Good fear. I also feared the inevitable punishment that I would receive if I disobeyed my parents. Good fear. Unfortunately, that fear was not strong enough to produce unerring righteousness, but it certainly helped enough to protect the neighborhood from destruction. I also came to fear the shame that my unrighteous actions would produce. Being the son of a preacher, I realized by the age of five that I was my father's richest source of illustrations, often to my embarrassment. Good fear, nonetheless.

From well-meaning people I suffered three direct spiritual fears in my younger days. Most of all, I feared missing the Rapture of the Church. No one ever assured me I would make it. Indeed, the question, "Would you want to be doing that when Jesus comes?" served as an effective preventative.

Fear of demon possession formed my second fear. Once again, boiling adolescence fell prey to the manipulation of different speakers. Whatever it was that I had or did must be a demon, according to them. I didn't know all the arguments against it then.

Finally, I feared that I might have committed the unpardonable sin. Once again, manipulative questions such as, "Are you closer to Jesus than when you got saved? Do you feel stronger about him now than when you were first saved?" were used as proof that something terrible must have happened in my walk with the Lord. My fear of God, until I came to truly know and understand him, was more like terror, knowing that someday I was going to "get it."

Eventually, with greater understanding of God, that terror gave way to respect and love. The statements of Scripture that support this: *For God hath not given us the spirit of fear; but of power, and of love, and of a sound mind.* (2 Timothy 1:7 KJ) and *There is no fear in love. But perfect love drives out fear, because fear has to do with punishment. The one who fears is not made perfect in love.* (I John 4:18) were statements that created some anxiety in me because of the clash of those statements with my terror. Finally, I truly saw Jesus, the Father and the Holy Spirit. The plug was pulled on terror. It was all so obvious and logical. The upshot of all of this is that I, now armed with greater understanding, determined to be an instrument of fearlessness in the lives of others.

Now, I realized that the only fear worthwhile was the fear of anything that might weaken or remove my relationship with God. This brings me back to my earliest statement about fear being such a motivator. The fear of a harmed relationship with God is not the greatest motivator of mankind; the fear of man is. Jesus warned us not to fear those who could merely harm the body, but those who could kill the soul. When I see men of faith purposely using fear about our future or livelihood to move and manipulate people, alarm bells go off in my heart.

We "religious conservatives" fall prey to many conspiracy theories, right and left. Fear generates an independent life for any perceived threat. My teenage years coincided with the McCarthy era when we thought communists were coming out of water pipes and lived in our attics. I recall a famous tent evangelist who promised to reveal to us the biggest communist in America, but we had to have tickets for that night, though they were free. He asked that we be discreet in sharing the tickets. Good ploy there.

After a forgettable sermon, he finally revealed whom he determined to be the biggest communist—Kate Smith, who sang "God Bless America" so beautifully. I went home that night with a fair share of disgust, but I also realized that the biggest fund-raisers at that time on Christian radio were those who effectively made us afraid of communists and who assured us that if we sent them an offering, they (imagine that) would lead the parade in stopping the devilish influx of communism. I wished that someone preaching the gospel would be so successful.

Further, I have discovered that the trend continues to exist. A procession of fearable opponents waits (always) just beyond the horizon to end our way of life. Food grown differently from horse-drawn plows will kill you. Be afraid. Water from your public source will kill you. Be afraid. Cholesterol will kill you. Be afraid. Lack of cholesterol will kill you. Be afraid. The Trilateral Commission will kill you. Be afraid. The Illuminati will kill you. Be afraid. UFOs will kill you. Be afraid. Angel-produced giants will kill you. Be afraid. Computers will kill you. Be afraid.

How long can this list go? Endlessly. Why do we cherish fear. What will be our next fear? Must we keep reinventing conspiracies? Or perhaps, live in the peace of knowing that God has made arrangements for us?

Long ago, I decided that I would no longer dedicate any mind time to such scary theories. I heard clearly the call of Jesus to come to him and he would give me rest. At least the Saduccees knew that he was afraid of no man. I long ago decided that my work was to obey his call and encourage and train his people. I long ago realized that my job was to be where people are and give them hope of redemption.

I invite you to rest in the knowledge of his care. Any current fear is meaningless compared to the glorious opportunity to be his agent among the people. Of all the people in the world, we have the greatest reason to be fearless.

Fear is being self-centered. Fear is bondage. Jesus' instructions were to "Go" and "Go unafraid." Let us be wise and prudent and fearless and free.

Feelings

Anyone who has bothered to observe the paradoxes of life knows that feelings and facts are strange bedfellows. At times they seem to be friends who cannot exist without each other and, at other times, mortal enemies.

From my own observations, I have decided that feelings are fickle critters that can't seem to decide where to give loyalty. If a huge truck is bearing down on me, the feeling of fear is a direct result of true and imminent danger; but when I detect no true and immediate danger and yet have feelings of fear, what does that say about the truth of the feeling?

Or, one can experience the opposite circumstance—a true and present danger without any feeling of fear. Here again, I must ask about the truth of the feeling.

Compounding this struggle further, feelings, fickle as they are, become terrible tyrants when they are the rulers of our lives rather than mere providers of information. For this reason, we must somehow rule them in order to establish their role in a healthy way. The whole subject is a morsel larger than this column can chew so let's narrow the confines to our opening subject.

To what degree can we trust our feelings about God and things spiritual? Perhaps I should deliver some further definitions according to Erwin before we continue. I believe that feelings are the results of many things, but truth may or may not have anything to do with them.

Truth, to me, is Jesus himself as the living Word and the Bible as the written Word. Facts are merely supposedly accurate bits of information about the world. Feelings are our emotional responses to information, truth and experiences.

With those definitions, let us propose some situations. What if my friends are planning a surprise birthday party for me, and, as I notice what seems to be strange behavior, I become angry and think they are doing something bad. Regardless of my observations, the truth of the matter is different from the reactions of my emotions. Consequently, I must call my feelings liars.

Suppose I feel that God doesn't love me or that he is getting even with me. The truth is that God is love and that he is forgiving, thus my feelings do not represent the truth and are lying to me.

Does this mean that feelings are not real. No. Feelings, though real, are neutral (neither good nor bad) but they are not always accurate. When they do not reflect what we know to be true, i.e., Jesus and the Bible, then we must be brave enough to call our feelings liars and act out of what we know to be the truth rather than our feelings.

God is Compassionate, Merciful, Slow to Anger, Abounding in Love and Faithfulness, Forgiving of Wickedness, Rebellion and Sin. (see Exodus 34:6,7) Regardless of how I "feel," I choose to believe those truths about God. Consequently, I will demand that my feelings conform to that Truth.

Competition

Without competition, much of what we know in America wouldn't exist. The "free enterprise" system has competition as its underpinnings. Sports would not likely exist. Competition is used to motivate the learning experience in schools. Competition is so much a part of our success and part of our cultural experience and has been so successful as such, that we assume it to be a most profitable method to bring into the body of Christ. That is where the scheme falls apart.

Though fine for our society, competition, by its very nature, strikes at the heart of the church. In society, competition assumes the core of evolution theory to be true—survival of the fittest. However, in the body of Christ, we have been taught by our master that even the least is greatest, thus our carnal systems of choosing winners are inaccurate and damaging rather than edifying.

When I speak of this subject, I usually get a swift and occasionally negative reaction. I notice, however, that the negative reaction never comes from those genetically excluded from the "winner's circle" of life—those we call "losers." No, the reaction always comes from those we would consider to be "winners." These winners see competition through different eyes. However, in the eyes of the kingdom of God, all redeemed people are winners and whatever systems we devise, we must convey that message.

The Foot Bone Knocked Down
the Ankle Bone

No body can survive with parts competing against each other. A body is designed to be healthy when each part is doing its job in a thoroughly cooperative manner. Since we are the body of Christ, this speaks directly to us. Competition, by its very nature, is self-serving—the very opposite of the servant, self-giving nature of Jesus. Some specific attributes of competition prove our case.

For competition to work there must be a prize—either a material one of value or else the prize of simply proving mastery over others and being number one.

First, to seek a material prize as the result of doing the work of God is to misunderstand or disobey Scripture: *For the kingdom of God is not a matter of eating and drinking, but of righteousness, peace and joy in the Holy Spirit,....* (Romans 14:17)

Second, to desire to be master over others is to disobey the injunction to be last for the benefit of others. To seek and achieve a position over others is to feed one's pride. Without pride, the achievement of being better than others would be meaningless.

Because of the value of the prize and our drive toward it, competition tends to give rise to cheating. Rather than fostering the best attributes, it brings out the attitudes that go along with the spirit of materialism and pride.

I have discovered that I am a poor winner. When I have bettered someone, I gloat. I can't help it. It is the natural me. Sometimes, in "friendly" kidding, I will remind the loser frequently of the fact that I have beaten him. I can become rather obnoxious.

But if I am a poor winner, I am an even poorer loser. After losing, I ransack my storehouse of rationalizations. My feelings of jealousy and resentment toward anyone who would be so arrogant as to defeat me run rampant. From the moment of the loss, I enter the scheming phase—planning for that moment when I can even the score. It dawned on me one day that the attitudes I had in both winning and losing showed little Christlikeness.

Another problem of competition is that it can measure only the least significant of our actions. One can never give a prize for spirituality or faith or love, because these attributes cannot be measured. Instead we measure specific physical actions like the number of visitors brought to Sunday School, or the most money collected for our project, or the most verses memorized.

Every contest has to have rules. Who decides the rules? Someone comes up with a set of rules depending on what action the rule-setter desires. This arbitrary method guides our lives whenever we are involved in competition. We faithfully abide by the "rules."

Perhaps the biggest problem for the health of the body of Christ is that competition creates so many losers and so few winners. To belong to Christ is to be a winner as far as eternity is concerned. Any activity that does not enhance that reality but instead reinforces the common human feeling of being a loser does not fit within the pattern of the nature of Jesus.

Can It Be Redeemed?

I do believe that competition can be rescued. I'm sure there are more, but here are six ways that can move competition within the body of Christ into kingdom values:

1. Avoid prizes that elevate winning to detrimental levels.

2. Create competition that equalizes genetic differences. If all you play is basketball, the tall guys always win, for instance. But if you have to shoot from midcourt all the time and shoot backwards or play blindfolded, it matters not how tall you are.

3. Create competition that makes ignorance or evil the opponent rather than the other person the opponent.

4. Create work that makes cooperation and fellowship the winner rather than beating someone the goal.

5. Since giving is so important to the Christian lifestyle, create giving competition. You will really need creativity there!

6. Devise means of giving the ...*less honorable* (parts)...*special honor.* as Paul indicates in 1 Corinthians 12:22-25.

Church Athletics

Church sports leagues have a stained record as far as the kingdom of God is concerned. Seldom do you find church sports leagues to be the place where kingdom principles are most likely to be displayed. As a pastor, I canceled an entire sports program in a church because the events regularly occurring on the field were opposite to what I was teaching about Jesus. When it was reborn several years later, a new set of attitudes prevailed.

In the new system, the treatment of people was more important than the scoreboard. Whoever came out for the sport played in every game, frequently to the detriment of the score; but the score was secondary to the people. I was pleased with the new approach, but it took effort to keep it pure.

Other teams looked forward to playing us even though we might win, because they simply enjoyed being with our team. League officials visited the church just to see what had fueled such a "Christian" view of sports.

During the process of working through this problem, I wrote a creed for the Christian athlete. Here it is:

Athlete's Creed

I am a follower of Jesus Christ and a member of his body above all other memberships.

In all activities I will seek to build and strengthen the body of Christ.

I will seek recreation that grows out of fellowship and makes fellowship grow.

I will seek to follow kingdom principles in all areas of sports and will esteem others better than myself.

I will operate in my recreational activities in such ways that everyone will win regardless of the score.

I will play as if Jesus were both my teammate and opponent.

Clues from the Bible

What does the Bible have to say about competition? It is clear that we are in a race, but it is against Satan and evil, not against our brother. *For the weapons of our warfare are not carnal but mighty in God for pulling down strongholds, casting down ar-*

guments *and every high thing that exalts itself against the knowledge of God, bringing every thought into captivity to the obedience of Christ.* (2 Corinthians 10:4,5 NKJ)

This verse requires our action in the public arena to be unassailably Godly. Meeting Satan on his turf does not mean meeting him with his own tactics. The world will always beat us when we play with their methods. Our only victory will come when we fight or compete with the weapons that the world cannot comprehend, thus cannot defend against. Notice, in any political race, that no candidate has to spend any time defending himself against righteousness, only rumors of unrighteousness.

Of course, we must decide whether competition is carnal or not in order to choose how we will use it. Another verse gives us a clue: *For we do not wrestle against flesh and blood, but against principalities, against powers, against the rulers of the darkness of this age, against spiritual hosts of wickedness in the heavenly places.* (Ephesians 6:12 NKJ) I hope it is obvious that I am not saying to abandon all competition. Indeed, we are in a wrestling match; however, I am saying we must abandon all tactics that will not glorify God. If you are a businessman, you cannot avoid the obvious competition of the marketplace, but you can avoid the dishonesty and the immorality. You can work to be the best you can be and strive to let your light shine so men will see your good works and glorify the Father.

So, we are in a battle, but whatever methods of warfare the world would naturally use would fall into the area of the carnal. Our energies must go into the realm beyond the flesh so that we can win eternal victories, not just temporary ones.

The Final Straw

The Scripture loads backbreakers on the question of competition among members of the body of Christ. For instance: *Let nothing be done through selfish ambition or conceit, but in lowliness of mind let each esteem others better than himself.* (Philippians 2:3 NKJ) This verse doesn't support some of our current competition, does it? It does support a method of competition that we seldom think about—to compete to see who can lift others up the most.

In another Scripture, Jesus bypassed an obvious opportunity to affirm competition:

> Now there is at Jerusalem by the sheep market a pool, which is called in the Hebrew tongue Bethesda, having five porches. In these lay a great multitude of impotent folk, of blind, halt, withered, waiting for the moving of the water. For an angel went down at a certain season into the pool, and troubled the water: whosoever then first after the troubling of the water stepped in was made whole of

whatsoever disease he had. And a certain man was there, which had an infirmity thirty and eight years. When Jesus saw him lie, and knew that he had been now a long time in that case, he saith unto him, Wilt thou be made whole? The impotent man answered him, Sir, I have no man, when the water is troubled, to put me into the pool: but while I am coming, another steppeth down before me. Jesus saith unto him, Rise, take up thy bed, and walk. And immediately the man was made whole, and took up his bed, and walked: and the same day was the Sabbath. (John 5:2-9 KJ)

Can you see the competition going on beside that pool? The question facing the whole crowd was "Who gets into the pool *first* when the water is troubled?" I see them crowding around. I feel the tension among them. I see them jostling each other for the best position. This competition offered the highest prize. But where was Jesus? Did he trouble the water? Did he encourage the competition? No. We find him walking in the fringes and finding a man who could not compete. That was the man he healed. The secret of Christian life is to look for Jesus. Where he is we must be also.

Some Final Conclusions

Is there an obvious set of conclusions? I think so.

First, we should adopt an attitude of never competing against our brother in kingdom matters.

Second, we must never, never institutionalize competition within the body of Christ.

Third, if we choose to bring competition into our activities, we must work hard to redeem it—make it prizeless, fun and equalizing.

Fourth, if we must compete in the marketplace against the world, we must never abandon Christian principles. It must be recognizable that we are trying to glorify God and can be trusted to be free from the bondage of fleshly methods.

Fifth, we must work hard to fully develop our capabilities so we can lay them at the feet of Jesus and let him anoint them for use in his army.

In the meantime, let us work shoulder to shoulder.

Everything You Need

If you love God, you unquestionably want to have everything happening in your life that God wants for you. This will certainly mean having the overflow or filling or baptism that marks the promise of the Holy Spirit. Maybe you have begun to long for that kind of lifestyle. The question: Is this available for us today? I think so!

However, in the event you feel as yet unimpowered, let me offer a simple approach to the overflow of the Holy Spirit. God responds to the hungry, seeking heart. He does not force himself upon us. We hear his voice and we choose to follow him. (John 10) There is no other way.

Jesus gave us a pattern for prayer in what we call "The Lord's Prayer." After opening with our honoring (hallowed) our heavenly Father, the next words are "Thy kingdom come." Those are very personal words from a hungry heart. We literally say, "God, dominate me. Be in charge of my life."

Then Jesus authorized us to pray, "Thy will be done in earth as it is in heaven." His will is certainly for his children to be filled with God himself. To prove just how available he is, Jesus, in Luke, Chapter 11, makes three overpowering statements. First, Jesus tells of a man unable to offer hospitality to a visitor who arrives at midnight, so he goes to a neighbor, awakens him and asks for bread. In spite of initial resistance by the neighbor, he receives everything he needs. Because hospitality was an absolute, a village responsibility, a necessary given, in the culture of these villages, the neighbor knew he would get the bread. It was a foregone conclusion.

Next, Jesus states, *Ask and you shall receive, seek and you shall find, knock and the door will open to you,* even promising that everyone who asks, seeks, or knocks, succeeds. In other words, it is a foregone conclusion.

Finally he teases his listeners with some no-brainer questions: *If your child asks for food, will you give him a rock, a scorpion, a serpent?*

The answer is "Absolutely not." Then Jesus reveals the subject of these three illustrations—the Holy Spirit. *If ye then, being evil, know how to give good gifts unto your children: how much more shall your heavenly Father give the Holy Spirit to them that ask him?* (Luke 11:13 KJ) In other words, to those who ask, it is a foregone conclusion. God will not withhold the Holy Spirit from those who ask.

The only limitation seems to be the *everything-he-needs* statement. The Holy Spirit is not a personal thrill trip or merely an experience, but is, instead, the executive presence of God to fulfill his servant-hearted, others-centered will. The thrills and experiences are there in keeping with Scripture, but the greatest joy for us and Jesus is to do his will. That is where the power of the Holy Spirit concentrates. So, God's invitation has arrived. It awaits only your response.

RSVP

1. Focus your attention, your study efforts and your praise on Jesus himself. In other words, fill yourself with the knowledge of Jesus and believe on him. (John 7:37-39)

2. Invite the Lord to empower your life and overflow you with the Holy Spirit for the benefit of others.

3. Believe and accept that he is now working in your life. Since all God's gifts are received by faith, you can trust that he will answer this prayer.

4. Watch to see what new events will happen in your life, what new power will be there, what new understandings, what new energy for service, what new drive toward purity.

5. Do not close the door to the miraculous or to new experiences if they match Scripture. Be bold and watch God work.

6. Pray for boldness to speak God's word and ask God to heal and *perform miraculous signs and wonders through the name of...Jesus.* (Acts 4:29,30) In the Early Church, God responded with an overflow of the Holy Spirit when this prayer was prayed.

7. The Holy Spirit was also given as a down payment in our lives to assure us of our salvation. (2 Corinthians 1:22 and 5:5) If you lack this sense, ask the Lord to reveal this reassurance to you. Then

just enjoy watching what the Holy Spirit is doing in your life.

8. Pray more and more unselfishly. Discover the promise that the Holy Spirit also prays in our behalf in keeping with the will of God. That cooperation unlocks great power. (Romans 8:26, 27)

9. Abandon fear. With the Holy Spirit in your life, you have a restful assurance of God's relationship to you. Enjoy it! (Romans 8:15, Galatians 4:6)

10. Prepare to know him more and to be more like Jesus because of the action of the Holy Spirit in your life.

Fine Dining

God has placed himself in you and has gifted you by his Spirit. As the Apostle Peter exhorts us in 1 Peter 4:10, *Each one should use whatever gift he has received to serve others, faithfully administering God's grace in its various forms.* So, if you really want to enjoy being God's child, place yourself in situations where you will truly have opportunity to serve and grow. This does not mean abandoning larger gatherings, but you will find that your greatest growth and fulfillment comes in smaller home-type fellowships. As you meet "in his name," you will discover he is truly present.

For the decades of my life, I have enjoyed watching the Holy Spirit provide growth in my life by keeping me strongly attached to Jesus the Vine. I have marveled at the miracles I have seen because he was at work. I have wallowed in the joy of his presence.

I stand amazed at how God takes my failures, anoints them and makes them his successes. I gloat in the rest he has placed in my soul. I hunger for the same for you. He responds to hungry people. Welcome to the table. Let's eat!

Home Groups That Work

BENEFITS OF A SMALL HOME GROUP

1. They are small enough for people to know each other.

2. Everyone can participate rather than be spectators.

3. The home is more comfortable and informal. Neighbors are more likely to come.

4. No investment is needed to function.

5. The Early Church seems to have used this pattern.

6. They bring Christian activity to where it belongs.

7. They are an effective method of "salting" a city neighborhood by neighborhood.

8. They equip people for ministry.

9. Everyone can pray and be prayed for—minister and be ministered to.

10. They bring accountability to our lives.

11. They are a powerful source for personal growth.

HOW DO I BEGIN?

Pray for the Holy Spirit to guide you and bring the right people together to begin. Make a list of those you think are interested and invite them. Do not pressure or push anyone. After you have the commitment of a few (and it may be a while before it happens), arrange for your first meeting and at that meeting choose a future meeting time that best fits the schedules of all concerned.

WHAT SHOULD THE MEETING ACCOMPLISH?

Successful groups have developed some common patterns for the meeting. It must deal with current needs. It must be personal. It must provide stimulating, applicational, disciplined search into the Scripture. It must be a time of communion when people share themselves and needs are met. Eventually the Holy Spirit will move you to ministry beyond your group.

HOW SHOULD THE MEETING BE CONDUCTED?

Here are some guidelines:

1. Keep the meeting informal so all will feel at ease.
2. Sing together—preferably easily remembered choruses. Informality dictates that you sing with guitars or without accompaniment.

3. Let each individual report on his previous week—a time of sharing the current action of God in your lives. This can include reports of intense needs and prayer which will move you quickly away from superficiality.

4. In the first meetings give an hour to a different person at each meeting to tell their life story with the leader going first. When that person has finished his story, each other member of the group should relate a positive item that they noticed about the person from his story or something that they appreciate about the person.

5. Pray—conversationally, specifically. When specific needs are expressed, take the time to pray for each one of them. Avoid generalities such as, "Pray for my loved ones." A response to this statement (and others like it) could be, "How do you want us to pray and for which loved one?" Realistic, specific praying will produce exciting sessions later as reports come of God's answers.

6. Study the Bible—applicationally. Study portions that deal with principles that can be put into effect in your lives. Or study the passages used in a recent sermon. Guidelines for applicational Bible study and enough questions to take you through your first meetings are included at the end of this chapter. Additional questions of this type are in the study guide of **The Jesus Style** by Gayle Erwin.

7. Make a commitment to meet for two or three months and keep it. At the end of that time, you can re-evaluate your commitment to continue.

WHAT SHOULD THE LEADER DO?

The leader is the key to group growth or failure. Here are some rules to help:

1. Don't dominate the group. You are a guide to see that everyone participates and that the discussion stays reasonably within boundaries the group has agreed upon.

2. Remember that you are a fellow discoverer of God, not the authoritarian deliverer of all truth.

3. Keep the discussion personal, practical and experiential. Avoid opinions, debates and impersonal theological discussions. You want people to apply the Bible to their lives; consequently, you will find yourself asking this question often: "How do you apply that in your life?" or "How have you experienced that principle or that verse?"

4. Don't attack people or permit them to be attacked for weakness or poor statements. Trust the ability of the Holy Spirit, the Bible and loving relationships to shape and mature people.

5. Set the pattern for openness, honesty and acceptance. If you stay on surface matters and cliches, so will the group. But if you are honest with your needs and insights, the group will be, also.

6. Don't probe into each other's lives. Don't give advice (preach). Don't judge others about their actions or openness. Keep confidential what is shared. Don't interrupt (for exceptions, see #8). Listen intently to each other.

7. It is your task to see that each person has opportunity to speak. If one person tends to dominate, ask him privately to give others more time.

8. If someone gets off the question, break in at a pause, thank him for his comments and say, "Now, let us get back to...."

9. You can expect some problems. That is part of life and growth. Not all groups succeed. When a group becomes ingrown, loses sight of its purpose, fails to be flexible, fails to keep Christ as the focal point, has one individual who dominates, fails to keep confidences, or fails to develop a loving interest in each other, then it is in trouble. If, after weeks of being together, people continue to hide their true feelings, the group is in trouble. You will need to openly and honestly face your problems if you wish the group to continue. There are times when the group should not continue (if the commitment level is low or the group becomes a gossiping or divisive group, etc.) and that should be recognized.

10. Don't worry about entertainment. Any refreshments should be kept simple.

11. Don't be afraid of periods of silence. These may be productive times.

12. When your group grows above 12 in number, divide the group and give birth to some more home groups. A group may discontinue upon the completion of a major ministry project, perhaps with individuals giving birth to new groups.

APPLICATIONAL BIBLE STUDY GUIDELINES

It is important to guide participants away from opinionizing and into application. What do I mean by that? Here is an example conversation with my comments. The subject is Romans 12:1, ...*I urge you, brothers, in view of God's mercy, to offer your bodies as living sacrifices, holy and pleasing to God—which is your spiritual...worship.*

Participant: I think that "bodies" means the fleshly side of man and this means that everyone in the church should really strive to be holy.

Comment: He is stating an opinion that may or may not be correct. At any rate, there can be two sides, and usually, if there are two sides, someone is going to take the other side and you have a debate going. The leader's job is to get away from the theoretical and back to the personal and practical. Here is a sample method.

Leader: Thank you for your comment. You may be right, but tell us what you see as fleshly in you and how you have become more holy. In what ways have you experienced this verse?

Comment: If he hasn't applied this verse to his life, he has no right to impose an arbitrary opinion on the rest of the group and this system gently brings that out. Now, just because he hasn't experienced it doesn't mean that he can't comment. If he admits that he hasn't experienced it, then the leader's next statement would be something like this:

Leader: If you see this verse speaking to you, then in what specific ways do you feel you need to be more holy or what do you personally need to sacrifice?

Comment: The leader is keeping the discussion centered around how the individuals can apply the Bible to their own lives. These sessions must avoid sermonizing and giving advice. We are free to share what God has done in our lives through the Word or what we feel he is going to do because of some insight we have gained, but we are not free to impose our interpretation on others. The Holy Spirit must take our testimonies, coupled with the Word, and do his own work in their lives. The main jobs of the leader are to keep the discussion in the practical and see that everyone participates and no one dominates.

APPLICATIONAL BIBLE STUDY QUESTIONS

Applicational studies basically ask two questions: "What does the Bible say to me?" and "What am I going to do about it?" To assist you in your studies, here are 12 sets of applicational questions:

NEW CREATURES
2 Corinthians 5:17; Galatians 6:15;
Colossians 3:10

1. Tell how you became a Christian.
2. These passages speak of freshness and new-ness. What "fresh and new" things are happening in your life?
3. What are three things you like about this new person you are?
4. What is God still working on in your life to make it new?
5. How do your friends think you have changed?

FORGIVEN
1 John 1:8-2:2

1. When you became a Christian, what did it mean to you that all your sins were forgiven?
2. Describe how God is helping you realize your forgiveness.
3. What role is confession playing in your life now? Read James 5:16 and describe how this verse has affected you.
4. When do you feel cleanest before God? Think about the fact that Jesus is your defense attorney and tell what that means to you.

WORSHIP
Matthew 22:37,38; Psalms 150;
Revelation 4:8,11

1. Write down as a group all the words you can think of that describe God.
2. Describe in two or three sentences what Jesus has been to you today.
3. If you were free to express your praise to God in any way you wished, how would you do it?
4. Try "counting your blessings" to your group. Let them share in thanking God with you.
5. The first time you see Jesus face-to-face, what do you think you might say or do?

PRAYER
Matthew 6:9-14, 7:7, 18:19; James 5:13-16;
1 John 5:14,15

1. When do you find yourself praying the most? When is it and when most difficult? What tends to get in the way of your praying?
2. What are some recent answers to prayer you have received?
3. What improvements in your prayer life would you like to make?
4. What experiences have you had in "agreeing" with someone in prayer and receiving an answer?
5. What prayer would you most want God to answer now?
6. Recite the "Lord's Prayer" together as a group.

THE BIBLE
2 Timothy 3:16; Romans 15:4; Acts 17:11

1. Describe your personal Bible reading practices.

2. What are some of the Scriptures that have been most meaningful to you?

3. What Scripture is going through your mind at the present?

4. What changes, if any, are you willing to commit yourself to in your Bible reading for the next week?

5. What Scripture do you wish you understood better?

GIFTS
1 Peter 4:10,11; Romans 12:6-8;
Ephesians 4:11-14; 1 Corinthians 12

1. What do you do that you think helps others? In what ways do you find yourself being helped by others? Can you see any connection between the help and gifts?

2. List all the gifts you found in the Scriptures above. Which ones do you feel you have and which ones would you like to see operate in your life?

3. Everyone is gifted. How are you trying to fulfill your gift and your calling?

4. One at a time, let each person in the group be silent while the rest of the group shares how they feel the silent person is gifted.

THE ROYAL LAW
John 13:34,35; 1 Corinthians 13; James 2:8;
1 John 4:7,8

1. Name some people you believe have really loved you.

2. List some of the ways you like to be treated.

3. From your list in the previous question, which ways are you doing the best in treating others and which ways are you doing poorest?

4. Jesus said to love your enemies and pray for them. Without using names, share what you would pray for someone who might be an enemy.

5. Love reveals itself. Tell the group how open and honest about yourself you feel you have been with them.

MATURITY
Ephesians 4:11-14

1. What are some of the main things you feel you have learned since becoming a Christian?

2. What spiritual fads or doctrines did you once believe that you have moved away from?

3. What do you feel Jesus is teaching you about himself right now?

4. What would you like to learn from God that could help you be more productive and at peace?

5. Who are you helping to learn to serve and what is your process of such discipling?

FRUITFULNESS
Ephesians 4:11-14; John 12:24; John 15 and 16

1. Describe three people other than your parents who have helped to shape your life or have influenced you.

2. Who was the "John the Baptist" who prepared the way of the Lord for your life?

3. For whom are you trying to be a "John the Baptist" and bring to the Lord? How are you doing it?

4. Who are you helping to mature? What methods are you using?

5. In what other ways do you feel you are attempting to produce fruit?

SERVANTHOOD
Philippians 2:5-11; Matthew 18:1-5, 20:25-28, 23:1-12; Mark 9:33-37, 10:35-44;
Luke 9:23-25,9:46-49, 22:24-27; John 13:12-17

1. If you were to make a list of people who serve selflessly, who would be on that list?

2. From the Scriptures above, build a list of servanthood or "greatest in the kingdom" traits. In

which of these do you feel you are strongest and weakest?

3. For each of the other members of the group, state which of these traits you think is their strength.

4. If you were to "wash someone's feet" or serve them in some way, you would go to whom and do what?

EXPERIENCING GOD

Ephesians 1; Romans 12:1,2;
1 Corinthians 12:31

1. What biblical sacraments and events have you experienced, i.e., salvation, water baptism, baptism in the Holy Spirit, communion, prophecy, etc.?

2. Make a line chart of your spiritual history with its ups and downs and share the story with your group.

3. What experiences or gifts would you like to have from God? Have the group pray for you to receive.

4. How have you come to know the will of God for your life? If you are unsure of his will, explain to the group.

STEWARDSHIP

1 Corinthians 6:19,20; Psalms 24:1;
Romans 14:8, Matthew 6:33; 1 Corinthians 16:3

1. What systems of financial giving have you developed in your life?

2. In what ways have you found God meeting your needs when you have been faithful (or unfaithful)?

3. How much time do you usually make available to the kingdom of God after meeting your own schedule?

4. For what project of the body of Christ would you be willing to devote your energies?

Tourist or Teacher

Wisdom in Cross Cultural Ministries

In 1976, a missions organization sent me around the world to investigate their ministries to see if they were doing what they said they were doing. Because this organization wisely refused to send Westerners to oversee all its operations but instead chose leading people in each country to fulfill the vision, I decided to call it an "incarnational" type of ministry. I will use this term often so I must now define it:

DEFINITION: Incarnational Ministry—A ministry in which you try to put yourself in someone else's shoes to understand his feelings and circumstances before you act. A ministry that protects the dignity of the recipient. A ministry to equip the recipient rather than establish dominance over him.

Because of the attitude this missions program had established, I was treated to unusual honesty from its workers in foreign countries. This honesty shocked me and confronted most of my mission misconceptions. I did not know then how valuable and useful that information would later be.

In 1978, an interesting twist of events, resulting from my classroom teaching on the nature of Jesus, caused me to be invited to what was then Rhodesia (later Zimbabwe) to speak at a national renewal conference. Though Rhodesia was deeply segregated and in the midst of a civil war, this conference was to be an integrated one at least as much so as their situation and understanding would permit. Since this would be my first experience before such an audience of Africans, I asked an evangelist friend from Kenya to hear what I planned to say and tell me if it would be appropriate.

After listening attentively, he said I would be the first White man they had ever heard say this and they would love me. He proved to be correct. Rhodesia was a flashback to extreme segregation days in the USA. It seemed that every racial attitude that I had heard expressed in the Deep South of the United States 30 years ago was given extreme form in Rhodesia. While there, it dawned on me that the stance taken by the White Rhodesians (and anyone else in a prejudicial racial stance) placed their eyes, ears and brain in a form of bondage that I call "White Think." Since I will use that expression again, it must now be defined:

DEFINITION: White Think—Thinking that judges others only through one's own culture or skill or race. (Note that the color in this definition can be changed.)

Being a firm believer that I am a member of the kingdom of God before I am a member of anything else, it seems to me that all forms of thinking (imagining?) must be brought into submission to the nature of Jesus, especially if I am to cross cultural lines, so that the message is not destroyed by the messenger. That belief, along with my travel experiences and my strong adherence to the nature of Jesus as basis for all actions, has brought me to some observations that I feel are almost indispensable for the mission-hearted person. These observations and the resulting principles have been tested and affirmed by Developing-Country leaders.

I can assure you that this understanding and practice can save you time and embarrassment and protect the future of the Gospel wherever you go. I believe the desire to go overseas represents genuine mission concern and the raising of funds for a missions tour is a valid expression. Thus, hopefully, the points to follow will make your involvement profitable.

Assumption #1: I can find my ministry in a foreign country.

If you have not developed your capabilities and proven your ministry here at home, do not expect that you can do so over there. To be a tourist and observe might be appropriate, but to go to another country to "find" your ministry is to become an instant burden to them. First of all, your thoughts are inward as you still develop and find yourself and you are unable to be truly others-centered. Second, you absorb their energies as they try to figure out just what to do with you without hurting you. Just because you are White does not mean that other countries welcome you with open arms. Most countries will not give you a long-term visa unless you have skills that are needed and in short supply. The kingdom is not in short supply of people trying to "find" themselves.

Assumption #2: I can evangelize the Developing World.

The problems? First you must learn the language. Most of the world speaks a language and writes a script very foreign to the average Westerner. To learn the language becomes a gargantuan task and you will not likely ever be fluent enough to effectively preach in the language. (It can be done with proper commitment.) Second, the sheer time required to prepare and move is a precious commodity unnecessarily lost. Third, you must still learn the culture and learn to incarnate effectively. Fourth, you must overcome governmental and cultural resistance to "Americans." Fifth, if you are Caucasian, you must somehow overcome the circus caused by your white skin. Sixth, you must raise an exorbitant amount of money each year to support yourself as an American. These are all unnecessary (for the most part) problems. For what it costs to send one American, 50-100 native workers can be supported and they already know the language and the culture and have managed to have the correct skin color. So, if I go overseas, I may be able to help someone else evangelize the country but I will not likely be able to do so myself.

Assumption #3: Developing-Country people are ignorant of the Scripture.

This may be true in many cases, but to assume the people are ignorant will cause you to treat them in a patronistic way and will quickly shut their hearts away from you. When people go with me overseas and ask me what they should preach, I tell them to preach the best sermons they would to their own congregation—to teach the finest lessons they have available. They should simply adjust by taking out all slang and idiomatic expressions or references to things specifically Western. If God has given you a special message for your life, go prepared to share that. Your studies should be completed before you go. The places where absolute ignorance exists will not likely be the places of your ministry. Most of the world is not open to our evangelism; however, they are open to our teaching their leaders and equipping them to do the work.

Assumption #4: Developing-Country people are ignorant, period.

It is true that many things we know are not part of their education, but they are as intelligent and learned as we are in their own way. Once again, to see people as ignorant savages (consciously or unconsciously) is to patronize them and shut the doors of their hearts to us. In our brashness, others often wonder why we are so ignorant of what seems to be simple courtesies and how helpless we are without our house full of technologies.

Assumption #5: Our technology and prosperity make us better than others.

Arrogance and racism seem to be part of the natural fallen state of man. We automatically assume that because we have more automobiles, better roads, working telephones and a multitude of technological gadgets that there must be something inherently better about us or that God has given us "most favored nation" treatment.

A truck driver once shared some wisdom with me that I have not forgotten. He said, "Education doesn't make someone a better person. Education will not keep you from killing someone; it will only keep you from eating him after you have killed him." If we understand that technological advancement has enabled us to sin with greater skill, then we are more likely to appreciate the relational skills of the less technologically advanced person and be more likely to learn from him.

I have heard Whites put Black Africans down because they would not try to "get ahead" in life. They (the Whites) would say that the Blacks might plant more corn but they would then let their hungry relatives collect from their fields and thus could not store up a lot for themselves.

The bottom line in this thinking is that they would never have a bank account or own a TV set at that pace. Until one is in a different culture whose values are shaped by different expectations, one cannot fully know his own prejudices. When we begin to get perturbed or outright angry at other cultures because they don't have what seems to us to be obvious efficiencies, then we have come face-to-face with our values. We who say we are citizens of the kingdom and students of the Bible discover quickly that we are also bondslaves to American prosperity and efficiencies.

True, we have prospered in the United States—some say by divine right and blessing although their theology doesn't seem to explain the prosperity of "non-Christian" countries. But prosperity is a dangerous and deceptive state. It quickly places us apart from others making it easy to violate the "no reputation" approach of Jesus. Frankly, it makes us a bit arrogant when we discover that we make more money in half a day than the average person in a Developing Country makes in a month.

What values would a person develop in the absence of money? A foreign trip helps one assess these values. Also, you discover, in the absence of the gadgets of prosperity, just what is necessary to happily survive. One must, if he is to be honest in his Christianity at all, devote some time to the study of the teachings of Jesus about money and prosperity and the direction of the heart before visiting a poorer nation. One must also clearly hear the words of the Apostle Paul in 1 Corinthians 8:1, *Knowledge puffs up, but love builds up*. I have yet to be able to correlate with Scripture the belief that a Christian is a better Christian because he has money or because he drives a posh car or because he has a sophisticated stereo or because he can direct dial his mother.

Assumption #6: Developing-Country people should submit to us when we go to their countries.

Again, this is an arrogant and unchristian attitude. Before we go to a foreign country, we should ask ourselves a basic question: "Just what is it that I am going to share with this country?" Am I going to teach them about American football? Do I want to teach them about how to date like American lovers? Do I want to teach them how to build buildings our way? Or, hopefully, do I want to teach them about God and his Word?

If I say that I want to teach them about God and his Word, then I must carefully peel away all tendencies to teach them something other than this. It is a devastating experience to take the time to compare my own values with those of the kingdom of God. Most Westerners go to foreign countries because they have been contacted by another Westerner in that country. The traveler then submits his schedule to the Westerner in the foreign country which endows the foreign Westerner with additional power—making others have to ask him for the services of a "desired" traveler.

A breakthrough came when I decided that in the White-run country of Rhodesia, I would submit my schedule to a Black church leader. Since Blacks constituted the vast majority of the population, I knew that true kingdom values would be better understood by a Black man. I told him that he understood the country far better than I and that he would have a better grasp on where I could go to bless the kingdom. If anyone wanted to have me preach at his church, he must go through the Black leader.

Sad to say, some White leaders who wanted me to speak for them approached me privately and asked if I couldn't come to them. I said that I thought the time was available, all they had to do was ask the Black leader since I had submitted my schedule to him. Some were unable to bring themselves to ask a Black man for the services of a White person.

To submit yourself to the local church and its leaders is one of the most affirming steps and relationship building actions you can do. Let me say also that I agree with the late professor Tom Brewster about how we should arrive in another country. He states that going to a foreign church is like being born into another home. Coming out of the airport is like coming out of the womb. A certain imprinting occurs, a bonding, to the people who welcome us out of that womb. If we choose to have Westerners meet us, then our bonding will not be with those to whom we will minister. Our ministry will simply be forays from the Western home into the other culture. We must be met by the local people or our ministry will always have a taint of "us" versus "them."

Assumption #7: Americans can easily learn the truth by observing or asking questions.

Most people who have lived under a colonial system or a system where they were governed by White strangers have learned to say to powerful people the things those powerful people want to hear. If you watched "Roots" on TV, you probably noticed the things slaves learned to do to cope with their owners.

That same spirit still exists: "Tell the White man what he wants to hear, but above all, protect yourself." Consequently, the White man, who loves to hear what he wants to hear, has great difficulty finding the truth. This is why Rhodesians, when their country changed to Black rule, were totally shocked when Mugabe was chosen as Prime Minister. The Whites wanted a man named Nkomo to be elected and the Blacks knew that was what the Whites wanted, so the Blacks assured the Whites that Nkomo would be elected while overwhelmingly electing Mugabe.

The intimidation of our wealth and position to a Developing-Country person is stronger than we can understand, and overcoming that wall to hear the truth is not easy. For instance, some "fact-finding" trips to South Africa by a very conservative TV newsman to investigate the scene there produced predictable results—a White man's conclusion about the Black man's condition. This reporter was either woefully unschooled about interracial communication or else had something to prove rather than to find. Even a White South African who was staying in my home took offense at the conclusions he heard on TV.

When I first went to Rhodesia in 1978, the White people were constantly telling me how the Blacks felt about things. When I managed to make some inroads into the Black mind, I discovered that the White people were almost totally wrong about what the Blacks thought.

The first reason for the discrepancy was that the Whites were more interested in control than they were in information. I discovered that White people never actually talked to Blacks and especially never listened to them. Questions by the Whites left room for only one answer. For instance, they might ask, "You are going to vote for Nkomo aren't you?" Obviously, the only safe answer to that question would be "Yes."

In order to deliver the truth, the person being questioned must feel totally safe in your presence. He must feel that you have some understanding of and sympathy for his situation. He must feel a positive regard from you. He must know that you are not going to be blabbing his answer to everyone else who might wish to question him. He must know that you have no vested interest in a particular answer.

There is no easy way to achieve a truthful situation except to adopt the "no force" or "gentleness" aspect of the nature of Jesus. First, one must study the situation of the person you are questioning. Second, you must put yourself in his shoes and understand what it would be like for you. Third, you must pass the test of close observation in your conversation and actions and exhibit a consistency in your action that lets him know you are not just using words to your benefit. He will watch to see if you ever defend his race as well as your own. Truth is a precious commodity.

Assumption #8: Developing-Country churches should adopt Western customs and buildings.

Often we take such care to be precise in our theology and are so careless in our practices. I have seen men far prouder that something "American" was happening than that the Word was being preached. To what am I alluding?

Where in the Bible does it tell us that churches should be organized like the United States government as some churches in this country are? Yet, we often are not satisfied until such occurs.

Where does the Bible tell us that all churches should be built like churches in the United States? Again, we are not moved unless we recognize that the building going up in a foreign country looks like a "church."

Where does the Bible tell us that we should be ruled by our wristwatches? Yet, we cavalierly jest at "Mexican" time or "African" time, etc.

Where does the Bible tell us that Western clothing speaks spirituality? Yet, we are morbidly enslaved to formal ties and suits and rest not until we have bound our poverty-faced brethren to such expensive but "clean" chains.

Where in the Bible does it tell us that our Western musical sounds are the norm by which all hymns must be judged. I often cannot believe my eyes when I read the magazines of evangelists and others who claim that they only feel the Spirit when our type music is used in hymns, this being adequate "proof" to them that all other musical sounds must be demonic. Incredible! What is the source of such arrogance? Is the fruit of the Spirit arrogance?

Then what is the action of one who understands that he is a member of the kingdom of God before all other memberships including citizenship of his country? Let me answer that by relating a conversation I had with Ezekiel Guti, a remarkable Black church leader of Zimbabwe.

I had just finished reading **Eternity In Their Hearts** by Don Richardson. Still deeply moved by what I had read, I approached Guti with questions about its accuracy and applicability. He listened as I explained Richardson's thesis and he quickly agreed. Guti said that the missionaries came to Africa and told the African that all things African were bad. Of course, the corollary is that all things "missionary" or "Western" were good. This immediately established a superior/inferior relationship and made it necessary for one to cease being African once he became Christian. This had been a major complaint also in China during missionary days. It was said that every time Christianity gained a convert, China lost a son.

Guti related that when he went to Israel for the first time and learned ancient Jewish customs, he realized that the customs of Zimbabwe—the ones that were supposed to be so wrong—were amazingly similar to those of the chosen people of God. He was glad to make this discovery but angry that the missionaries had not informed him. He felt that evangelism in southern Africa would be nearly complete now if these similarities had been affirmed rather than attacked.

A PLAN

What then is our goal of action? We must go with a heart that affirms more than it seeks to correct—even if our ways may seem more efficient to us. Efficiency of time may be a terrible steward of relationships, and Jesus seemed to be on the side of relationships. It is far more important to communicate love than technology. Because people of Developing Countries have come to think of themselves as inferior to us, affirmation from us has a great impact on them and quickly welds relationships. Even actions that seem humorous to us may fulfill a real need to them and we should not mock them.

Their phones and other "conveniences" frustrate our direct-dialing fingers, but it is their proud best. We damage the kingdom when we speak ill of what they have or joke of their idiosyncrasies especially in their presence, but also in our private conversations. Once we adopt, even in private, a jocular stance about them it spills over into our dealings in dangerous ways.

Assumption #9: Developing-Country people cannot be trusted with money or leadership.

This assumption has caused much pain in our relationships with other peoples. When it comes to money, we quickly fall into the heresy of thinking that there is an "American" church and there is an "Indian, African, etc." church. We begin to think that it is our money going to their church. Not so!

We are the body of Christ and members of the kingdom of God and we are one. It is all God's money—kingdom money. While it is true that other peoples are not accustomed to handling large sums of money as we prosperous Americans are accustomed to handling, it does not follow from experience and honest observation that we handle such large sums any more spiritually than they would. We tend to use God's funds to build monuments to ourselves rather than to meet the needs of people and of evangelism and when such funds are used for people, we feel that it has been wasted.

The fact is that our job is to equip people to do the work of the ministry. That, by its very nature, means teaching and trusting people with that precious commodity that tells us "in God we trust." The problem that I have observed is this: We get quickly corrupted by the power we wield when we go, with our wealth, into a people of poverty.

When I discover the amount of "control politics" we have played with our excess funds, I get disheartened. This is one reason why the word "missionary" has become an insult in many countries.

So What?

So, what is the answer? Simply to work alongside the people where God has sent us in order to equip them and quickly turn the reigns of power (money) over to them to do the work. Of course, this means also to teach generosity so that the work will not be dependent on our funds forever.

On the subject of leadership, let me build a scenario to show the inherent problem of cross-cultural ministry. A missionary goes to a foreign country. When he leaves his own country, the missionary is a poorer sort, perhaps on the poverty level by American standards. However, when he arrives at his destination, he discovers that he is at the top of the elite with his income. He is now the rich man. His funds give him power and he is held in awe and treated with the deference that any rich man would have anywhere.

Since money is dominant, why shouldn't English also be dominant as a language? So, the locals are taught (if colonial, they are required to learn) the English language so they can communicate with the missionary. Church leadership naturally goes to those who learn the English language best, since English is the focus anyway. The locals know that the best English speaker is not necessarily the true spiritual leader, so corruption has immediately begun.

Another scenario has the person among them who most successfully adopts the American style of leadership as the one chosen by the missionary as the church leader. This immediately ties Christianity to the United States and restricts its success to the feeling of the country toward America. I suppose the fact that we have so much trouble discerning who the true spiritual leaders are in our own country would naturally mean that we wouldn't know how to teach discernment in a foreign country.

So, what is our response? To incarnate ourselves into their culture, discern and equip their leaders, then affirm them in their leadership by submitting ourselves to them.

Assumption #10: They are as happy to see us as we are to be there.

We often go to foreign countries simply because we can afford the trip. The church in those countries often takes care of us simply because they can't afford not to. What do I mean by that? The first statement is obvious and needs no explanation. The second is less apparent. The Developing-Country Christian operates in an information vacuum. He knows less about us than we might know about him. When we arrive, he often has no way of knowing just who we might represent. If he thinks we represent supporters of his or are friends of those supporters, he may be afraid to limit entertainment since that may be more costly to his support than the destruction of his schedule is to the present work.

Once, several years ago, I visited with a national Christian leader in a certain country. His work was very effective but also very hectic. He seemed overloaded to me, so in my efforts to "help" him, I asked him what job of his took the most time in his schedule. His answer left me subdued: "Entertainment. You are the 15th foreign visitor I have had this month."

Sometimes, keeping an American for a period of time places a pastor under surveillance by the police or other authorities or shackles him with a reputation that might be damaging in his circumstances. In India, a worker was hesitant to take us into his slum ministry area because it would identify him as being supported by Americans—knowledge not to his benefit.

I have decided to always assume that I am a burden and do everything that I can to lighten that burden. Don't go unless invited and pay your way at the front end of the stay, not at the end. Often I have seen church leaders thrown into disarray by the insistence of Americans on some convenience that the Americans considered basic but that the local leaders were totally unable to provide. A sensitive heart will assess as quickly as possible what can and cannot be done, and even more important, what should be done.

Assumption #11: The United States government is the best and the most honest.

To paraphrase a couplet by Alexander Pope, "'Tis with men's cultures as his watches. None runs alike yet each believes his own." I have learned that, to be effective, one must go to a foreign country as a member of the kingdom of God and not as an American.

You will discover that foreigners have a different view of our greatness and honesty. It is true that our wealth causes every Developing-World person to dream of coming to the USA, but it is also true that we have not always worked in the best interest of other countries. Do not make assumptions that all people should be happy with us and do not be upset when you find strongly negative articles and editorials about the United States in foreign newspapers. Read them. It will give you a better perspective on the whole world scene.

Actually, if we objectively read our own newspapers as if we were visitors in our own country, we might be humbled a bit about our own corruption.

Assumption #12: Communism is the greatest threat to the world.

Though this is a bit outdated now, it seems to me that when the word "communism" is mentioned, an American's eyes glaze over and he loses his capacity to think. He now only reacts. Many Christians once got worked up by energetic anti-Communists and gave more money to fight Communism than they gave to spread the Gospel.

Am I opposed to Communism? Certainly! I am very glad to live in America with the freedoms available here. However, I fear materialism and its effects on Developing Countries far more than I fear Communism for them. Once the availability of "things" locks onto greed, the Church is in greater danger than from persecution. I have observed the corruption that money has brought to churches and it breaks my heart. I also notice that persecution seems to purify the church. So, my conclusion? The kingdom of God is the most important, not the spreading or fighting of anyone's government.

Assumption #13: A raised hand means a conversion.

Desperate for results or for egos to be massaged, we become prime targets for misunderstanding and even fraud. In naiveté, we do not know that hands are raised out of kindness to us, or because they know that to raise the hand will keep the money flowing to their country. But at least it blesses us and we get to show pictures and be excited.

I was once invited to a certain country to conduct crusades. Although I am internationally unknown and was certainly unknown in that country, the inviter asked me what size crowd I wanted. Whatever number I wanted could be delivered to me. I came away from that conversation a little wiser in the ways of the world.

In one country, I know that a "crusade" goes on all the time and is designed to dupe unsuspecting "supporters" into thinking that their contributions are producing great results. I have also learned that "instant orphanages" spring up to pry loose the American dollar. How can we know that what we see is true? It is not easy. The only way I know is to find a local or international ministry with integrity and let them be your eyes and ears and don't do anything to subvert their authority or findings.

OBSERVATIONS

Now that I have shared my reactions to this set of assumptions with you, I must record some observations that will, I believe, make any short term foreign missions trip more effective.

Observation #1: A camera is a wall.

Every tourist wants to return with good photos of the trip and that is fine, but when you are dealing with people, a certain dynamic enters that you must take into account. A camera makes performers out of people and makes them self-conscious. A camera traps people in a human zoo and you are the visiting observer. A camera also removes the photographer from participant to observer.

Suppose you are in a church service with local people and you have joined them in their fervent worship of God. When you take up the camera to record the event, you are no longer a worshiper, and you distract them from their concentration on God. If you choose to photograph worship times, be sure that the people in charge are comfortable with it and work hard to be invisible. Keep in mind when you ask for permission to photograph, that the answer will often be "yes" even when they mean "no." Learn to ask questions in a way that will get you the truth such as, "When people take pictures of you, how have they used them and have they ever been a problem to you? Do you wish you could put some controls on photographers? What would the controls be?" A sensitive listener will get much information in the answers to this type of question.

Remember also that a camera is an instant testimony of wealth. The average camera that we carry with us is worth several months' salary to the person we are photographing.

One other comment about photography: I have observed White missionaries taking photos of the ministries of native workers and coming back to the USA to show these as ministries of their own and using them to raise money for themselves. When the news got back to the native workers that this had been done and they knew the missionary had nothing to do with their work, the very appearance of a camera represented exploitation to them. One who photographs needs also to be very wise.

Observation #2: Giving your address to anyone who requests is not wise.

On the surface it would seem that to share your address with a person in a Developing Country would be an act of friendship and, of course, it can be; however, be very sure that the relationship you have developed with the person necessitates the exchange of addresses.

Normally, when you give your address to someone simply because he asks for it, you will be regularly sent letters asking you for funds. Of course you will have no way of verifying the need or the wisdom of sending such funds and you have placed yourself in a dilemma. You may ultimately not answer the letter while your foreign correspondent pays a day's wages writing to you.

So what can you do? Since you are likely to be in that country under the auspices of someone from that country or some specific organization, ask the person who wants your address to send any letters to you through your local contact or through the organization. This serves two functions. It makes any letter you receive by that route a serious one (you will not likely receive any letters this way) and it does not subvert any authority structures that might be in place.

Observation #3: Purchasing gifts to take home can be a damaging act.

If you are buying a group of small symbolic gifts that represent the country to take back to people who have an interest in your trip, then it should work fine. Often I will bring back a number of small representative gifts to give to people to remind them to pray for the country. But, you will discover that bargains do abound in some countries and you feel that you cannot pass up some valued purchase that would be exorbitant in the USA and now you can get it for half price or less.

Here is the problem: the cost of your purchase may represent a year's salary for the common person in most countries. To flaunt that kind of purchase could seriously affect their view of you and of the kingdom. It could be a source of discouragement to them. So, what can we do? First, be very judicious in our buying.

The kingdom of God is not made up of bargain buying. Keep the good of the people and the country in mind first. Large purchases, if they must be made, should be made as privately as possible and not flaunted in any way. If you are taking small things back to help people remember to pray, it compliments people to know you are doing this.

Recently, I ran across another problem in gift buying. Most Developing-Country markets thrive on the bargaining process—a process we Americans are unfamiliar with and largely uncomfortable with. We simply hear a price and decide "yes" or "no." Bargaining with purpose in a foreign market can be a fun event and a creative part of the trip to give you the flavor of the country.

However, if you are looking for native crafts and you ask local co-workers to bring you something made by Christians, be prepared to pay the asking price—you are no longer in the marketplace. Be prepared to at least buy something even if you feel the cost is beyond your plans. An example of what I mean: Some visitors noticed a certain type of very useful craft work of the local people. They asked their hosts where they could get such an item. Informed that it was all handmade and that women from the local church made them, the visitors asked to have some brought to them for purchase.

The lady who handmade the crafts left her job the next day and by bus and walking delivered a number of the craft items to the visitors. The visitors, upon hearing the price, looked the items over as if they were at a garage sale and decided they didn't want any of them and walked away.

Here are the things they didn't understand: The materials to make the crafts were costly in that country though they could have been purchased for less here in the USA. Second, they cost the person a day on her job which she was willing to sacrifice just to bless the Americans. Third, these were more than a mere product, these were items made by a committed Christian and faithful supporter of the kingdom. Fourth, by knowing the story of who made them, these items would have become even more valuable and a prayer and contact point for the country. Fifth, they were saying more with their brash rejection than they realized.

When I saw what was happening, I quickly bought almost all of the products that had been brought, ensuring the worker that I was deeply grateful for all the loving work she had put into the items. Seeing the tension of the scene, I knew immediately that the money spent would be small compared to the damage the rejection to this fine Christian would cause.

Observation #4: Western customs can be offensive and vice versa.

A discovery often made too late is that dress codes of the USA are much too lax for most Developing-Country Christians. If you are a woman, be prepared to wear only dresses or skirts—slacks and jeans are unacceptable. Men, be prepared to wear slacks and ties or suits except in casual circumstances when open collars are acceptable. In some areas, jewelry, including rings, are offensive and one should be alert to that possibility.

Many forms of Western humor are lost with other cultures, but one must be careful of humor anyway. Most humor is hostile in that someone must be the brunt of the story in order for it to be funny. Developing-World sensitivities do not permit the casual putdowns common to the American scene, so smile a lot and avoid jokes and most humor unless you are putting down or laughing at yourself. People appreciate it when Americans confess and laugh at their own foibles.

Male-female relationships are universally more structured in other countries than in the Western world. Usually it is inappropriate to have public shows of affection. Dating is taboo in almost all places, so teaching concerning dating would be offensive. Husband-wife relationships are often differently structured by custom, so one must be quite careful in teaching about marriage—careful to use biblical teaching and examples rather than American examples. Men and women often sit on opposite sides of churches in Developing Countries and do not talk to each other or touch in public. Do not assume that because hugging has found growing acceptance in the USA it is equally acceptable in foreign countries—especially when men and women are involved. As a man, do not attempt to shake hands with a woman or even touch her unless she reaches out to you.

In many cultures, eating with one's hand is the standard and acceptable way. Almost always, one would eat with his right hand, because the left hand is reserved for personal cleanliness functions. This "right hand" usage has some other effects. When giving or receiving gifts one should always offer and receive with the right hand. This may mean nothing to you, but it often does with others and it is easy to be alert to this practice.

In some countries you will see men walking together holding hands. This will grate upon the sensibilities of the American male, but in those countries, it does not have the same meaning that it would in the USA—it is only a mark of friendship and is completely acceptable. So, men, if you succeed in building friendships, be prepared to hold hands.

With the advent of the internet, research on customs is readily available, so take the time to do advance studies.

Observation #5: Wasteful duplication is common in missions.

Every denomination that I know of seeks to establish only its own programs in a given country rather than determine what is happening in an area and support, or enhance or complement it. Instead, if there is a Bible school with 15 students in a community, another denomination (often with almost identical doctrine) may come in and start another school right beside it. Wisdom and stewardship would make us careful not to further duplicate ministries in the kingdom.

Sometimes (no, often), ministries run by Americans will "buy" workers away from local situations just so they can tell how many they are supporting and thus get more funds from America. For instance, if someone is only making $25.00 in his current position (which might be quite enough by local standards) it is relatively easy for us to offer him $30.00 so that we can say he is ours. We neither won him to the Lord nor trained him, but now he is ours by purchase. Usually this will neutralize him in the eyes of his own countrymen and cost him years of ministry once he has discovered that we are not always dependable. I am amazed at how carelessly we hold people hostage with our wealth. Obviously this practice is corrupting and damaging to the kingdom.

Observation #6: Americans are often loud and crude.

When I overlay my culture on another country, I find that I talk too much and listen too little. Often I subvert the local leadership by trying to make contacts and develop associations with people I should not and with whom I cannot maintain a relationship. Having a friend in the West, especially one who sends or brings you things you requested (especially money), represents power. Such connections thwart the authority of the local leaders and inhibit the development of that person.

Because we might feel comfortable with a prob-ing investigative style in the USA, we will probe into personal or financial affairs in the presence of other persons. You will find yourself being avoided there-after.

I have seen money held back until buildings were built to Western style or painted in colors pleasing to the Western eye or moneys accounted to Western standards (without the benefit of comput-ers or training). We hold people hostage in more ways than we know.

A little-known way we hold people hostage is in paying their way to conferences around the world. Suppose, for instance, we are going to have a pas-tors' conference or some regional international Christian gathering. We benevolently decide that we will pay the way of a person from each Develop-ing Country since we know that they cannot afford the trip. The next question is, "How do we decide who that person is?" Much bitterness has grown in these countries, because we tend to choose some White missionary in that country to tell us whom we should sponsor; and the missionary will choose someone obligated or submitted to himself rather than a true representative or leader from the coun-try.

Observation #7: To find a ministry of integrity and effectiveness is finding pure gold.

There are so many paper organizations and phantom orphanages and invisible evangelists that we can easily fall prey to deception. To carefully check and verify a ministry and to build proper relationships and to thoroughly prepare yourself for foreign ministry is like finding the mother lode of a gold mine. When you have found a ministry of integrity and the Lord moves you to participate in it; pray for it, support it, give yourself to it and then dip into the incredible joy of watching the kingdom of God grow—knowing that you had a part in that ministry.

Observation #8: We can be too self-sufficient and not let them serve us.

As a tough American male, I can carry my own luggage and know how to fix my own breakfast and mow my own lawn. In my first intimate encounter with a Developing Country, I almost fought with the people to carry my own bags only relenting when it was obvious that I was going to lose. People would even rush up to me and take my Bible from my hands to carry it as I walked along. Finally, after one of my attempts to carry my own things, I was gently informed by a leader that I was keeping them from having the blessing of serving if I didn't let them help me. I don't know why I had not thought of that.

On another occasion, when I was ignorantly complaining about the vast difference between White and Black salaries, I declared that if I were living in the land I would not hire someone. I would do the work myself rather than pay them such a low salary. Again, a leader gently informed me that if I did so, I would be considered stingy by the local people and they would wonder why I wanted to deprive them of a job. Embarrassed by my lack of understanding, I resolved to listen harder and think clearer.

What can we do?

First, we can travel to learn and be more sympathetic and understanding and supportive. Second, we can be profitably involved in individual conversations. Third, we can share our knowledge of the Bible and certain practices with the workers. Fourth, we can have our "White think" prejudices confronted and brought into submission to the nature of Jesus. Fifth, we can, by being people lovers, help change the concept that people have of some bearers of the gospel. Sixth, we can, by our affirmation, increase the confidence of local workers and thus improve their ministries. Seventh, we can return and help enlarge the vision of the evangelization of the world in the hearts of our friends. Eighth, we can give. While we are prosperous and have the funds, we can give. This day of prosperity in the United States is not a time for stinginess, it is a time for generosity. Ninth, we can earnestly and capably pray once we have seen the mission scene. Tenth, if God has definitely said for us to "go," then we must go, but go with full knowledge and humble hearts so that our missions efforts match the nature of Jesus.

For more information on native missions support, consult Gospel for Asia, 1800 Golden Trail Court, Carrollton, TX 75010. 972-300-7777

Other Books and Resources by Gayle Erwin

The Jesus Style
A unique look at the real Jesus. In 30 languages and 42 printings, this hallmark book remains the book of choice for reading and giving to others.

The Father Style
This book breaks new ground in seeing God the Father through the eyes of Jesus. You will love him with all your heart.

The Spirit Style
The Holy Spirit through the prophecies and life of Jesus. A remarkably healing and resolving book.

That Reminds Me of a Story
Forty true and unique stories from the life and observation of Gayle Erwin. Taps the whole range of emotions.

That Reminds Me of Another Story
Gayle shares more of the richness of his life with 60 true and unique stories.

Video and Audio Tapes
Gayle's delightful insight and humorous approach to Scripture make these very popular to all ages.

To order or receive a catalog, write:
Servant Quarters, Box 219, Cathedral City, CA 92235
Or call toll free 1-888-321-0077
Website: www.servant.org
Email: gayle@servant.org

Gayle Erwin has spent 44 years as a pastor, college teacher, evangelist, magazine creator and editor and world traveler. He devotes his time to teaching and writing about the nature of Jesus.